MW01592120

The Transition

by Phil Ward

DORRANCE
PUBLISHING CO
EST. 1920
PITTSBURGH, PENNSYLVANIA 15238

The contents of this work, including, but not limited to, the accuracy of events, people, and places depicted; opinions expressed; permission to use previously published materials included; and any advice given or actions advocated are solely the responsibility of the author, who assumes all liability for said work and indemnifies the publisher against any claims stemming from publication of the work.

Dorrance Publishing Co
585 Alpha Drive
Pittsburgh, PA 15238
Visit our website at *www.dorrancebookstore.com*

ISBN: 978-1-4809-8758-6
eISBN: 978-1-4809-8873-6

To my grandchildren and theirs and others to come. I do not want them burdened with the same questions I had.

And to my wife of thirty-seven years, Jan, for her unwavering support and warmth.

To all my Combat Control Team brothers, past and present, and other SPECOPS friends from sister services, specifically Gen. John Singlaub, USA, Gen. William Byrd, USAF, Cols. Bob Reid and Lee Pitzer, Maj. John Gillespie. USAF, Capt. B.T. Collins, M.Sgt Skipp Minnix, 5th Special Forces, Sgt. Maj. James Tatum 10th Special forces, Sgt. Maj. Larry Smith, 22 SAS, Hap Saunders, Gary Harwell, Les Hall, Lou Brabham, Bob Kelly, Joe Hawkins, John Koren, K.B. Duncan, Art John, John Jenkins, Arlon Jahnke, Bill Winters, Hank Schaffer and Bill Warick just to name a few. They provided the resources for my transition

And, specifically, to an unnamed judge of the Criminal Court, Ponca City OK, 1951.

And finally to my close friend of seventy years and adopted sister, Joyce Jones, who has always offered support and love and who graciously agreed to proofread my effort.

Forward

Over my many years, I have been called many things, harassing, soft, obstinate, tough, relentless, brilliant, stupid, Republican, Democrat, Independent, liberal and conservative, sometimes all at once...as you will be.

But set your own course and listen to your own consciousness. Establish your parameters and protect them. Do not change your concepts or perceptions based on the moment, or events that are temporary.

As I was writing this, I suddenly realized that I had shorted you and left out the most important part. For it is not what we are, which changes, but how we got there, which does not.

This is my odyssey, written for my grandchildren when Chris, the submariner and the oldest of he and Nick, was born...if you're up to it, enjoy.

My father had deserted us when I was two. We were very poor and lived in a series of rentals in Cicero/Gurnee Illinois. I never had a bike and didn't realize until I went to High School that people had more than two shirts and two pants!

From 1936 to 1946 I was pretty much raised by my Grandparents and two uncles, AI and Doc. Grandma was my piano teacher, religious leader and teacher…and she loved flowers.

Except for Grandma, they were a drunken, violent bunch who often fought each for fun; but not in the house. Grandma did not allow that, nor spitting or swearing. If necessary, they would spank me with a leather strop, used in those days for sharpening a straight razor.

And this is what they taught me:

- HONOR. They were first and foremost an honorable group. They stood their ground, even when the majority were against them. In Grandpas eyes, giving up was cowardice. I never saw any one of them cheat or lie. They talked the talk and walked the walk. Their word was their bond and at Grandpa's funeral, many well-wishers told me stories of his fidelity.

- BRAVERY. On several occasions I saw them do brave things. My Uncle Doc once threw a man through a screen door for making fun of me. Grandpa rescued a small child from a raging bull. AI grabbed a burning Xmas tree and took it out the second floor window. In the early 1940's, they stood for a black family that was moving into our town, arguing that his family could live where they wanted. We all went out to their place and spent several weeks clearing the brush so he could plant. Grandpa once told me that "lying is for cowards, brave men do not lie." I was afraid of snakes until Grandpa caught one and forced me to put its head in my mouth and bite down. He told me that "fear is all in your head and if you look at it, it will disappear."

- EDUCATION. None of them had finished high school, but they all insisted I read books. They would bring them home from somewhere. I was allowed only one hour a day to listen to Buck Rogers, The Phantom, The Lone Ranger and others, and after Grandma had finished her chores, she would sit by an old potbellied stove and read to me from Defoe, Dickins, Bronte, Chaucer, and Ibsen. I understood little but it obviously gave her pleasure. She often said that she hoped I would go to "University."

- RESPECT. You respect your GOD, "kin", teachers and your friends because they are trying to help you grow up. Friends are more valuable than Gold

- RESPONSIBILITY. Be responsible for what you say and do. If you are wrong make it right. Hurt no one unless the cause is right. If you hurt them, do it well.

- UNDERSTANDING. They thought that I needed to understand people and events, even at my young age, so they taught me:

1. Do not trust what people say, only what they do.
2. If you are wronged, get even. Do it so they never forget.
3. Be afraid of no one, to do so allows others to control you.
4. Lying is for cowards.
5. Two people see the same thing but tell different stories, be careful of stories.
6. Most people will do anything to help themselves, not others.
7. Always do your best work.

This is the way I raised you, do the same for your kids

—Grandpa, Feb 1998

Contents

The Very Beginning

I was born in 1934, in the Waukegan Illinois Hospital. My father, Philip Edward Yeagle, I was told much later, had with his family, immigrated from England just after the first World War. The family allegedly settled in the Philadelphia area where they became involved with the furniture business. My father was reported to have enlisted in the US Army and was eventually assigned to Fort Sheridan, about fifteen miles south of Waukegan Illinois. Upon being discharged, he went to work on the North Shore Railroad repairing the seats and various upholstered fixtures.

He learned to play the saxophone well enough to play in a local dance band. In fact, this is where he met my mother, who played the violin in the same band, in 1931. They were married in 1932 and two years later I showed up.

Mom was an accomplished violinist who had played first violin in the Chicago Philharmonic. She played gracefully and with much movement, but always in time—the fingers of her left hand dancing on the frets, with a slight smile on her face. In the late 1920s, in one of the bands in which she played, was a new unknown singer, Perry Como.

She later told me, with stars in her eyes, that he even took her to dinner once. But that was the end of the romance.

In 1936 we had moved in with my Grandparents and, several months later, my father left us. It was reported that he was playing his saxophone on a tour boat operating between Tampa, Florida and Venezuela. Several years later a mutual friend told Mom that he had died in South America. Years later, when I became a private investigator, I returned to Waukegan for a visit. I spent several days attempting to find my father. Strangely, neither the U.S. Army, the railroad nor the musicians union had any record of him. The State Department had no record of his visa or his death. I questioned my Mother, her relatives and friends closely and found they all verified that he had worked for the railroad and that he played in a band. Strange indeed. My preschool years are hazy, but I recall playing with a few friends, one of whom was Donita Babcox, and the other was Eddie Heveren. Donita lived right down the street and was my constant buddy. Eddie's father was a close friend of Al's and he lived on the other side of town. I had a few others, whose names escape me, but Donita and I remained friends for many years until I left Gurnee. It was generally a pleasant time in my life.

And eventually I turned six and was judged old enough to walk the two miles to school, generally joining other kids also going to the same destination. Throwing stones in the creek, pushing and shoving but always smiling at each other. We enjoyed each other immensely as children at that age do.

For some reason, as we were crossing the small bridge over the creek, Donita had a habit of punching me or Eddie. So one day Eddie hid underneath the bridge and as Donita was poking me, jumped up and we both poked her. She ran home crying but that was the last time she bullied either of us. She taught me a valuable lesson!

The school was a small single-story four room building, a little country school, three of the four rooms held several classes and the fourth was for the teachers. The playground was to the side and had a swing set and teeter-totter. When lunch hour arrived all the kids with their lunch bags would gather at the swings for an impromptu picnic. During the winter, lunch was in your seat and small bottles of milk were provided.

If it was storming, Uncle Doc would give me a ride to school and pick me up. Once in a while, during spring, Doc would whisper to me, "I'll meet you this morning". That was his signal that I was to wait, out of Grandma's sight, behind a large oak tree and I would skip school. He would pick me up and we would go fishing in the lakes region. Twenty miles or so to the West. I don't believe Grandma ever caught on.

Doc, short and stocky, had a spinal deformity brought on at birth, and got his nickname because although he could not participate in sports, he could still help the team by being the trainer. Al was 6'4", quiet, serious, and withdrawn. I never quite felt comfortable around him. Years later, when I was fourteen, he told me I was a failure and I would never amount to anything, and probably spend my life in jail. My grandfather was of medium build and height. He was a simple, direct, honest, and often violent man, who ruled his kingdom, except for the inside of the house, with an iron fist. His concepts were ironclad and unchanging. On weekends, he and my uncles would head for the garage, and were usually half drunk by midday.

The house we lived in would today be referred to as a duplex, two story frame, divided down the middle with the McCain brothers, the owners, on the other side. It was a nice house, with a warm and lived in look, with a large detached garage in the back and a dirt driveway that circled it. We had a furnace, but no air conditioning. We did have a potbellied stove in the dining room and, of course, in the living room, or as she phrased it "the parlor," stood grandma's old upright piano where I spent many hours at the keyboard. There was a small unlit root cellar, dirt walls, and floor that was reached from the backyard porch, complete with a non-functioning hand pump. And we even had an old outhouse—unused and smelly. The house, with a new address, 4151 Old Grand Ave, still stands.

And in the house was the boss, my grandmother. She was stocky, with thin wisps of grey hair on her face, white stubble on her chin, and she was my salvation, my one bit of sanity that I held on to. Thursday was her baking day. She would bake everything to be consumed next week, pies, cakes, and sweets. But she would wait to bake the bread until I came home from school, so I could help and learn. All extra pastries or baked goods were stored below the back porch in the root cellar. She was firmly convinced that all men should know how to cook and to clean house, but I never saw her husband or her sons help her out. To this day, when I cook chicken or make strawberry shortcake, I use her recipe.

When not cooking or cleaning, during the spring and summer, she would tend to her flower garden located behind the privy. She was a staunch charter member of the Gurnee Garden Club, once being elected president. On Sundays, grandpa would drive us to church. He would not attend, but spent the time smoking his pipe in the car. Grandma would force me to sing the hymns but I understood little. When we got home, it was time for my piano lesson. On rare occasions, Mom would accompany on the violin.

The summer that I was eight, they decided it was time for me to become a man. Grandma got serious about the cooking lessons, and started letting me actually do some of the mixing. The uncles supplemented my education by teaching me to play poker and blackjack. Grandpa taught me to shoot his twelve-gauge shotgun with my back propped up against a fence post and arranged for my sex education.

One day Grandpa took me down the street to visit Doc Smith, our old country doctor. We sat in his kitchen at the table on which sat a bowl of oranges and a strange tool, about twelve inches long ,composed of a cylinder, trigger, and a thick needle with slots near the point. Next to it I could see old photographs indistinctly. And Doc Smith leaned back in his chair, adjusted his glasses, and began.

"Someday soon you will stop playing with yourself and lay down with a girl. And when you do, you will get so sick you will wish you were dead. You'll wish you had listened to your Grandpa about girls. This is what's gonna happen", he stated. "Years ago," the Doctor said, edging his chair closer, "on the sailing ships that plied the great seaports, occasionally the sailors would go ashore and do it with a woman and this is what happened to them," he said, shoving the photos across the table. They showed blurry pictures of men lying on cots or bunks, with their trousers around their knees, their penises red and swollen. "They had contracted a disease called gonorrhea. There were no doctors then, and they had to fend for themselves. These men died a horrible death, in great pain. The only cure," he continued, picking up the long pointed rod, "was to insert this in their cocks and pull out all of the scabs, like this."

With that he picked up an orange, inserted the tool, squeezed the device which caused tiny blades to pop out, and he slowly pulled it out, making a tearing ripping sound, juice dripping off his hand to the table.

To this day I have never forgotten the sound of the blades tearing out the pulp of the orange. But apparently years later it did not prove to be a deterrent. It was the best summer I ever had, a high point in my young life.

The View from the Bottom

And now to my step father, Eddie Ward. Black curly hair, about five foot eight, 150 pounds, with a pugnacious grin, a violent temper and a limping gate. He was very proud of a twenty-two round that he still had imbedded in his right forearm and he often told about how his brother had accidentally shot him when they were boys in New Mexico. He had grown up in a rough mining camp where his father worked on the Santa Fe Railroad. Eddie was uneducated but smart.

He and Mom were married in 1940 and he adopted me, moving into a small second floor apartment in Racine, Wisconsin while he commuted on the train to his job in Waukegan, Illinois. It was not far from the shore, and in fact I learned to swim in Lake Michigan, as cold as it was. My best recollection was that Eddie seemed to love Mom, treated her with kindness, smiled at her a lot, and tolerated me. They had several friends, all card players, and on Friday and Saturday night there was always a card game, euchre and beer, in most cases. And at family gatherings, pinochle and beer, was the game. But always the beer. In 1942, he enlisted in the Army and went to the Pacific, returning in 1946. During this period, Mom and I lived with the grandparents.

Mother was in her early thirties, slim, attractive and with a fine lot of hair. She was always kind and considerate, and never once spanked or corrected me. Mom was a hairdresser and often did not return home at night, telling me that she would occasionally stay with friends.

One night, in October 1943, when I was nine, I had a very strange experience. I dreamt that I was standing on my window sill, in my pajamas, and was looking down at Grandma's rose bush, shivering. It was a cold morning, cloudless, no wind to speak of with some stars still faintly twinkling. As I raised my eyes I could faintly see most of the neighborhood. The sun was soon to rise. I spread my arms up from my sides willed myself to fly. I jumped and flew off the ledge soaring higher and higher to the point that I could see the high school, about a mile away! Years later while freefalling, I recognized the feeling of the air rushing past. I flew towards the school, almost overcome with fun and glee, descended and flew around the gravel pit I sometimes swam in, then climbed to a altitude and headed away from the gathering daylight, smiling broadly and giggling.

Looking down, I could see all of the familiar landmarks that I passed on my way to school. The overpass, the old people's rest home, Depke's garage and the little bridge of Donita's fame. Ahead I could see a familiar "T" junction where I would occasionally buy an ice cream bar after school on Grand, the street we lived on, and Always Road, a junction I crossed on my way to classes. Near the intersection was a fire; it looked like a large truck had come down Always and missed the turn, and ran right into the front door of the house on Grand Ave. I circled and could feel the heat from the fire. It buffeted and warmed me slightly. Scared, I flew back to my window and climbed back in bed.

The next morning, at breakfast, my uncles sat down and began discussing the accident last night "down aways from here on Grand." Doc said, "Apparently a gas truck had run straight into the house there. The driver and the woman in the house both died."

I was terrified, for I could not understand what had happened to me. I had thought, when I awoke that morning, that it was all a dream! Even at a young age, I told myself that it could not have been real, impossible, a coincidence! I had dreamt the whole thing!

It was not until I was a young teenager that I ever told anyone about my out of body experience and to this day I have a hard time believing what had happened.

When Eddie returned from the war, he was a violent, abusive, drunk who would beat either of us for no reason. I suspect now, after a lifetime in the military, that he was suffering from what is now termed PTSD. We hated each other and made no bones about it.

I begged Mom to leave him, which she did, but for only six days. He convinced Mom that the three of us could not get along in the same house. In fact, he mentioned the Allendale School for Boys, across the lake from our house, where we lived in a one bedroom walkup flat, me sleeping on an Army cot in the front room.

I have debated long and hard about this next episode, which has haunted me for seventy-five years because, like everyone, I would like my grandchildren, and others, to think well of me.

It was not until I was in my late seventies that I admitted this to anyone, and then it was to Jennette one night, and I cried at the telling. Several months went by carrying this load and I finally told our preacher, Mike Thompson the story, in hopes he could provide the magic potion to erase the issue completely and irrevocably, but he could not. It is still with me, every day.

But this is an autobiography and remembrances should be true and factual, both the good and the bad.

I turned twelve, I had stolen, lied and cheated almost every week of my life. I was, in the accepted term, a truant, uncontrollable.

In 1947, in our wanderings, we had moved to Lake Villa, Illinois to be next to my grandfather who was living in an old folks' home.

One afternoon I was sitting on the backyard steps of the house we lived in, and across our yard, in a neighbor's yard, was a small terrier, leashed to a stake in the ground. He was not barking or growling; in fact he was laying peacefully near his dog dish, watching me.

He raised in me such a rage and hate that I was shaking in the fury. I went to the garage and got a rope and a can of gasoline and set the gasoline at the foot of a tree in our backyard. Turning, I walked to the dog, tied the rope around his neck, disconnected his collar and dragged him whimpering to the tree.

I threw the rope over the limb and hoisted the poor animal shoulder high, tied him off and dumped the gasoline all over him. He cried in fear and his eyes told me what he expected.

Somehow a match was struck and held to his tail and the flames erupted in a roar which did not hide his screams of pain. I stood there, not four feet from that dog, and for the next fifteen minutes watched him burn to death…and I loved it. The sense of power and control over that poor animal was exhilarating and a new high. I felt invincible.

The police came, there was much hollering and apologies, but not from me. Mom paid for the dog. The officer warned me about my future and what it was to bring. Many years later, doing research as a private investigator, I found that this conduct was a significant event in the childhood of mass murderers.

I have no explanation for my conduct. I did at that time, and always have, loved all animals, especially dogs and have been known to get in someone's face if I think they are mistreating an animal. Only much later, after I had joined the service, did I feel the remorse and guilt that I should have felt all along. Pastor Thompson drew out a diagram relating to guilt, sin and remorse; I have it posted on my bathroom mirror, where I do penance every morning of my life.

And so it was decided. I packed a small bag, Mom borrowed Grandpa's car and off we went to Allendale to register. We met Dr. Thompson, the Director, who seemed kind and understanding and the registration went quickly, Mom kissed me goodbye promising to visit every Sunday (she rarely did) and off she went. Dr. Thompson had one of the housekeepers collect me and showed me to my new home and introduced me to the rules and regulations.

Allendale School for Boys

She introduced herself as Mrs. Donning, and as we walked explained the process.

"I have been here for two years and like all of my boys, you will be assigned a job, go to school and church on Sundays, and behave yourself. If you have any problems, tell me. Discipline is firm and determined by the staff members. It could range from restriction to transfer to a boy's detention home in Antioch, a nearby town." I found her description mild indeed. Discipline could be ordered by any of the staff and was swift and violent. Below the kitchen were three small rooms, five foot square with a four foot ceiling, no furniture or bed but a bucket, no toilet paper. They were referred to as the "meditation chambers." Boys would meditate for seven days. Last stop before Antioch.

At supper I was introduced to my sixteen housemates, two of which, Bill Henderson and his brother Phil, I would keep in contact with for many years afterwards

I found out later that if a paddling was necessary, it was administered by a tall gaunt English teacher, Bucky Loren, with his three foot paddle that had holes in it. No matter where he went he was always accompanied by his dog, a Collie, appropriately named Lassie, even to Chapel.

After supper, I went for a walk to look around. I ended up on the boat dock, where I could see, across Clear Lake, my mother's house. And I cried. I have never cried since, except for the dog.

Allendale was a privately held and publicly funded entity. It existed to take unwanted boys at grade school level off the streets and provide schooling and some motivation for them. It was constructed in 1929 and still exists today. A major change occurred in the 1970s, when three new cottages were constructed and girls were admitted. It was not fenced in, because there was no place for the boys to run to. I think in the two years I attended there were only two AWOLs.

It was a modern attractive facility on open rolling hills, with seven cottages, staff quarters, a small hospital, a fifty acre farm, and a complete grade school up to eighth grade with central kitchen, print school, gym, and Chapel. There was also a very small park and a boat house and dock, minus any boats. The boat was considered a safety hazard, not an aid to flight.

Each cottage was similar, two story brick, in the English Tudor design. On the first floor was a small kitchen, living room with carpet, and a bathroom with a large shower. The second floor contained the house-mother's quarters and the dormitory, military style. Each of us had a bunk, centered methodically and bolted to the floor, and a wall locker.

There were six windows on the second floor, all barred, but the windows could be opened. I remember, during the winter, putting oranges out to freeze. They were a treat and a rarity.

Our meals were prepared in the central kitchen and were horrible. First because they were trying to keep their overhead down, and secondly, because they did not care. All meals were delivered in a large pushcart, motorized by two boys.

Breakfast was oatmeal, every vegetable at supper was stewed tomatoes. Neither of these have ever been allowed in my house. Meat, if available was overdone. And cold. The salads were huge, and from our own farm. There was a lot of stew and beans and the food was plentiful. Luckily the milk was good and it was cold.

Saturday was our free time and we all loaded up on buses in shifts and made the trip to downtown Lake Villa. We were each given five dollars to spend. This country town consisted of one bar, a large grocery store, Kroger's I believe, a drug store, which was our drop off point, a park by the lake, and several small businesses. We were allowed two hours in town, most of it at the drug store or market trying to get away with whatever we could. I have often wondered why the town council allowed this. By coincidence, Mom and Eddie lived about a block from our drop-off point and I never saw either while we were in town.

Sunday morning we formed in the small park and marched to the chapel, which we all attended, including staff. Dr. Thompson, who was an ordained Methodist minister, gave the sermon with the assistance of our boys' choir. Sunday afternoon was also free and devoted to visits from family, for those lucky enough to have caring parents. Normally only five or six parents would show. The rest of us would play baseball, football or basketball, depending on the season, occasionally fight, and during the summer we would all swim and dive off the dock.

The teachers at Allendale also served as counselors for the boys. Those of us with violent or truant background were scheduled for a session three times a week, after school. I was assigned to the music and geography teacher, Mr. Bradford.

He was of slight build with a full head of blonde hair and a very calm demeanor. No matter what I said in response to his questions, he never once was ruffled or showed impatience. And so I played the game, contrite when I thought that's what he wanted, regretful on command

and a whole list of other emotional facets. But over time, his persistence started to dent my armor, but not much. Generally it had been a wasted effort on both our parts. When I left Allendale, I was pretty much as I had arrived, except two years older.

And at this point my grandmother became sick and after a short illness, died. Allendale, sadly, would not let me attend because their policy only allowed this if it was an immediate parent.

Otherwise, our free time was spent in wrestling with each other, reading in the library which was a requirement, listening to the radio in the cottages, or just goofing off. Oddly enough, there were few serious fights. Once a week we would, in the evening, have movies in the gym and the kitchen would make and deliver large boxes of popcorn.

And I was fortunate to have been assigned to one of the better jobs, the print shop, which operated six days a week.

We had a couple old flatbed presses and the typesetting, of course, was done by hand. The printer, Mr. Judd, had the same problem with his back that my uncle Doc had, so along with my normal duties I also "fetched and carried." He set the type and sleeved it in the press, I and two other "inmates" would actually run the press. The jobs we did were those ordered in response to local advertising and in addition, some would come from Allendale graduates.

And my hat is off here to these graduates. Many years after graduating, they would send money back to the school, to "help out", sometimes in four figures. They belonged to the Allendale Association, which I belonged to for several years but slid away from.

Time passed quickly and without a great many incidents. I did, however get caught smoking and it earned me three whacks from Bucky's board. I made many friends that I corresponded with thru the years, some dying in prison, others becoming very successful. And my first kind of sexual experience occurred there. We had a female history teacher whose son attended the school. She would wear low-cut button-up-the-front dresses, top buttons always undone, and on occasion bend over to help a kid. It caused a commotion, because we all jockeyed to get a chance to peer down her dress.

Floundering

Once graduating from eighth grade, my parents were forced by law to take me back. It was a very unloving and tense household, the apartment had only one bedroom meaning I had to return to my old cot. Mom was continually afraid that Eddie and I would get into it. I began to sneak out of the house and with friends, go to the grocery store and see what we could steal, smoking all the way there and back., sometimes drawing obscene words on the sidewalk.

And one afternoon it finally erupted.

I had asked Eddie if I could borrow his jacket to go to as dance and he agreed. When I left the dance, I had forgotten it and was now on the way out of the house to retrieve it. He came roaring down the stairs, fist raised, screaming at me. I turned around, picked up a telephone from the stand on the wall and raised it, saying "(expletive), you take another step towards me and I'll kill you!, Don't you ever hit me or Mom again, if I got to wait for you to fall asleep, I'll kill you then! Come on (expletive.), come on!" He turned and climbed the stairs.

After this incident, almost daily Mom pleaded with me to treat Eddie with more respect. And she was now pregnant with my brother

Jon. To Eddie's credit, after Mom got pregnant, I never saw him raise his hand to her.

From that day on Eddie and I were very cautious around each other, both trying not to upset Mom and walking on the shelf of hate we had for each other. We would not speak to each other unless it was an absolute necessity; and we would not stay in the same room together. In fact, it was not until I was in the service, years later, that we ever spoke at length.

They never had a house or car, always lived in dumps and hitched a ride or bussed it wherever they went. I never knew if my threat had an impact on him, but I believe that from that point on, he never touched Mom. And of course the birth of his son changed him a great deal. I had heard that he absolutely doted over Jon and gave him all he could manage. And apparently their marriage had stabilized somewhat. After I had joined the Air Force, they rented a fairly nice two story in Waukegan and lived there until after Jon graduated from high school. In fact, Mom no longer went to a shop, but did her beautician business in the house.

I left home when Jon was four so I never had the pleasure of really knowing a younger brother. Eddie died in the late eighties and Mom remarried, it lasting for several years. She lost her husband and then moved in with Jon. She passed away several years later at the age of ninety-two. I must say, everything considered, I believe she did the best she could and I loved her very much. In many ways, she was also a victim.

I started high school in Antioch, a town about fifteen miles north of Lake Villa. Every day I caught the bus with the other high school students at the drug store, and every night was dropped off there. Because of this, I could not participate in sports or after school activities. My year there was uneventful and boring, except for one instance. An old high school friend of Mom's had a daughter and they lived next to the football field. Her name was Janett. She was a little shy, a blue-eyed blond who was just developing a chest and I had met her several times and we clicked. On occasion Mom would offer to provide transportation and I would spend a few hours with them.

One Saturday her parents left for the afternoon and Janett and I found ourselves on the couch. I was able to get a feel of her breasts, but she absolutely refused to let me "go down there". Our relationship declined at that point. My wandering eye for the ladies, which was to get me in trouble for the next forty years, was born.

In June we moved to Zion, Illinois, again into a second story walkup, but this one had two bedrooms. Starting my sophomore year, I almost immediately found a girlfriend. Her name was Charlene, and she was a preacher's daughter. We would consummate our relationship in many ways in often strange places. In her father's study in the Church, in the backseat of the car with her parents in the front seat, in the park during daylight, ad infinitum. It lasted until I moved to Waukegan, a year later.

In Zion I had a chance to participate in sports and I played halfback on the junior football team. I was not good enough to play on the first string, but once in a while, the coach would take pity and send me in for a quarter. And no, I never got a touchdown or really helped the team in any way.

I had a friend, Bob Studebaker and he and I were constantly up to no good. His father was a dentist in town and late one summer, because we did not want to go back to school for our junior year, we put dental paste in all of the locks. It took them several days to get all of the locks changed Another time his parents took off for a couple weeks on vacation and the third night they were gone, Bob threw a party, which was great, boozy and glorious. I had my one and only marijuana cigarette, called, in those days, "Mary Jane." During the party, someone took

Bob's Mother's cat and stuffed it in the freezer. The next morning, lifting the lid, here was the cat looking up, frozen stiff with a snarl on its face...a long super summer!

In addition, here was my first exposure to gang violence. Zion was originally populated by religiously inclined folks from the East, who in the 1920s settled in the small town and rapidly developed several religious factions and edicts. In fact, no beer, liquor or theaters were allowed within the city limits, and it was known far and wide for its religious zealots. And I suspect one of the reasons for having so many churches was that there was a little known law that if you had one, you paid no Illinois, county, or city tax. It was not uncommon for someone to have a church in their home with only three or four members.

For some reason, in the mid 1940s poor southerners began to settle in the town. Because they practiced a different life style and had different beliefs, they were ostracized by many in the community especially by us teenagers. And so, gangs were formed.

I started "on the street" and as a result, there were a few fights, and during one I was hit with baling wire under the eye and had several stiches. My participation in the gangs and attendant pursuits increased. And I was becoming unruly with my relatives and my mother. I completely ignored Eddie's existence.

At fifteen we moved to Waukegan and I transferred to that high school. We lived in a small, two bedroom shack on a county road, on the outskirts of rural Waukegan. I, luckily, after a short search, found a part time job at the local airport working in a paint shop twenty hours a week, after school. By the time I turned sixteen, I had saved enough money to buy a 1939 Studebaker Coupe for $150, a wreck on wheels but it moved. And thereafter, I became part of the high school upper crust, those of us who drove to school.

And I met my bride to be, Alice. She stood five foot two, a little on the stocky side with a turned up nose and a nice ass. Alice traditionally wore tight sweaters and poodle skirts, then the fashion. She was an average student and only slightly disciplined. I tried as hard as I could, over the next few months, to "cop a feel", but the best I did was one night in a movie, I got one of her breasts which was covered.

She was living with Fred and Mabel Stuart and their daughter, Joyce, Her birth name was Young, but she had lived with Fred and Mabel Stuart in Waukegan, Illinois for several years and so occasionally she would adopt their name. I had met her in the fall of 1950 at, of all places, the church. A friend, Craig Thomson, had dragged me there one Sunday and I was immediately infatuated. She, her sister Joyce, and their parents, Mabel and Fred, were all church members. Fred was a school teacher, Mabel a housewife, and Joyce was a college student.

Fred was a contradiction in attitude and perception. He was first and foremost an educated man and an excellent teacher. But not far underneath lurked a man, profane, violent and abusive. His wife Mabel was tiny, white haired, long suffering, intelligent and very respectful of her husband. I'm not sure she loved him or perhaps was out of love. She was the kindest, gentlest and most caring women I have ever known. From the start, they emotionally adopted me, and in response, I tried to clean up my act so I would not embarrass them. And my ties to Fred, Mabel, and Joyce continued down thru the years, even after Alice and I were divorced.

Fred and Mabel had seen some tragic circumstances, loosing, I believe, two newborn girls, and a boy before birth. Fred told me years later that the loss of his son shook his marriage and his faith and something crumbled inside. He admitted that somehow, which he did not understand, he blamed Mabel for his son's death. The tragic loss of his son haunted him for the rest of his life.

I did not know Joyce very well. She was smart, beautiful, sexy and vivacious, with a serious streak not far below the surface, and seemed unhappy.

I had some interesting friends. Joe Sorenson, who ended up as a millionaire in Montana, Sammy Paprician who died in prison, Dick Hunt who was a carpenter, Joe Kennedy who became prominent in Chicago real estate circles, and finally the Broadway, movies and TV star, Jerry Orbach, who in High School was a little shy and withdrawn. After school we would all hang out at the pool hall, drink bear, swear, shoot eight ball, and during intermissions, go out and steal from stores what we could. Bill Henderson and his brother from my Allendale days joined up on occasion and we had some riotous and illegal times.

At one point, after we had hit a liquor store, Joe and Sammy got into it, and rolled down the stairs trading punches, unfortunately knocking down a couple people. The cops were called and we were all cited for being delinquent. I was a poor student and failing in my junior year. I had been fired from my job for stealing auto parts, and the pressures at home were unrelenting.

One morning, the Stude would not start and this pushed me over the edge. So, at age sixteen, I quit high school, said goodbye, "I'll see ya," to Alice, left home and began bumming around the Southwest, stealing, fighting and being "over the edge." One night, in a bowling alley, I got in an argument with a kid over bowling shoes and stabbed him. The next morning the judge gave me a choice of jail or I could join the military.

The Transition Begins

I enlisted in the USAF on June 14, 1951. I was selected for Air Traffic Control School at Keesler AFB, Mississippi. But I had not learned my lesson, for I spent four days AWOL in Room 401 of the Biloxi Hotel with a thirty year old Chicago teacher. Once that idyllic union got old, I got up from bed and went straight to the 1st Sgt. and turned myself in. For being AWOL, I was busted and served thirteen days in the stockade.

Upon being released, I was reassigned to another squadron so that I could re-enter training where I had left off. And behold, who was two bunks down but my old friend from Allendale and high school...Bill Henderson!

And so we reunited in mischief. We had a lot of fun visiting the various bars in downtown Biloxi, and teasing the girls, sometimes with interesting climaxes, if you get my drift. One night, half loaded, we decided to climb the base water tower, and did so, Bill chickened out half way up, but I reached the top and the view of Biloxi and the Bay was exhilarating. I shouted as loud as I could, "expletive, expletive, expletive!"

And I went home on leave and found Grandpa sick and dying. We had always told him that his drink would get him and in the end it did. He was crossing the street with his pail of beer and was hit, breaking his back. While I was at home, Eddie's attitude towards me seemed to have changed. He took me to his local hangout, introduced me and we partnered in a game of gin rummy. He was jovial and alert, and even kidded me occasionally. I returned to duty wondering if this change would last.

Grandpa died the next month and I returned for his funeral. As I have stated, the church was overflowing with his friends and acquaintances and there were flowers everywhere courtesy of Grandma's Club. Many approached me and told me stories of Grandpa's talents and reputation in the County.

In the course of our barracks life, we had one black guy. Archie Stone who was from around Kansas City, Kansas. He was a good-sized kid and had been a football star in a small town in the suburbs. And Archie was different from the rest of us in another way.

He was a Christian. In the 1950s Christians were rarely ostracized when they appeared in public, because in those days no one felt any differently towards Christians than any other religion. Of course, feelings about various races were constantly making the news .And in the military it was a rarity to meet a Christian, white or black. Archie, up to this point, had been attending the base chapel every Sunday. We would see him put on his civilian clothes, check his shoes to make sure they were glossy and at about 1030, off he would go. And punctually, at 1230 he would come through the barracks door, undress, neatly stow his "civies" and sit down in the never ending card game. It was usually pinochle and he would have a bottle of smuggled beer at his elbow, laughing and carrying on as we all did. And occasionally a pint would show up, but because of the cost, not often.

But this Sunday he announced that he was going to church downtown in Biloxi. Dressed and looking sharp, we saw him board the bus for the thirty minute trip downtown. We all thought we would see him return in a couple of hours.

An hour and a half later, he came through the door, obviously upset. He quietly, amid our questions about what happened, changed his clothes, laid on his bunk and would not talk to anyone. He avoided all of us the rest of that day.

Finally, on Wednesday, after Taps, Bill, who was his bunkmate, got him to talk to us. He had gotten off the bus a half block away from the old Methodist church and as he was walking up the steps, a group of young whites approached him and asked him what he thought he was doing. He replied he was going inside to worship Christ. They told him, in no uncertain terms, that "niggers are not allowed here and never show your black ass again," and he was shoved down the stairs.

There was stunned silence in the barracks and then began a slow rumble. As the word spread, the barracks erupted in anger. Bill was finally able to quiet everyone down and voiced his plan.

The next Sunday at ten o'clock, at the bus stop, were sixty-two airmen dressed in their best uniforms. We got off the bus, and in formation, with Bill calling the commands and Archie in the front rank, marched up the church steps, entered the church, and quietly sat in the last six pews. There were a ton of glances and stares from the congregation, and some mumblings. At the end of the service, we waited until all of the folks had left, we stood, formed up and marched out, four abreast.

The minister, of course, knew what had happened and he was extremely apologetic, in fact shook Archie's hand and invited him back.

Archie continued to worship at that church and eventually was invited to sing in the choir. He was the only black in the congregation.

And he never saw any of the group that had harassed him, eventually finding out that some of them quit going to that church, in protest.

In November of 1951, I graduated and received orders for Scott AFB, Illinois. I, being the lowest ranking airman, was assigned to work night shift in the DF (direction finder) station, which was a red and white silo in a field adjacent to one of the runways. Its function was to provide magnetic headings for lost aircraft, vectoring them to the base. The only frequency we could communicate on was 137.88 MHz, VHF. Communication with the tower was via telephone. We had no UHF, which was just coming in. It was a long and boring job.

There was, for some reason in the station, an M2 carbine with full magazine. To pass the time, I would field strip it eventually doing so in the dark. And the days passed slowly, and without incident. I was learning to keep my nose clean and attend to my military responsibilities. In fact, six months after arriving, I was promoted to my original rank. I was also selected to go back to Keesler for Approach Control School and completed it, placing third in a class of twenty-seven.

In 1952, I asked Alice, who was living at an adult care center in Chicago to marry me and she accepted. She had ended up there because the Stuarts, shortly before, had moved to Yermo, California where Fred was teaching in middle school.

I brought Alice to Scott AFB and we were married in the Fall of 1952, in the Base chapel. Alice was short and slightly stocky, literate and a fun personality. We loved each other deeply and without reservation.

Our first residence was an attic apartment across from the Bellville Hospital. From the start, it was a financial struggle. We had no car and the money I was making as an airman did not go far enough.

The bus fare to and from the base ate up a quarter of our income. In desperation I tried to hire out to pull others KP for ten dollars, but that was not quite enough. I finally found a part time job washing dishes in a diner near the house, ten hours a week for seventy-five cents an hour. I begged Alice to try and find a job. She said she was trying but not having any luck. I suspected that after I left for work, she did not search but went back to bed. And eventually I was proven right.

At one point, for several months, we would buy Cokes in a bottle on paydays, the first and on the twenty-second of the month, return them for a deposit and purchase four cans of chili macaroni. We subsisted on this until payday, For the first five month period, on the twenty-second I would hock my watch for ten dollars and on the first redeem it for twelve bucks. Luckily, I was promoted which meant I no longer had to hock my watch, or do KP for others. But we continued to return the empties and eat chili mac the last few days of the month and my dishwashing career continued.

In 1953, our first son, Mike, was born in the hospital across the street. He was a big baby, a bouncer and cooler and gave us little problems. Alice was attentive and always there for Mike. She suddenly seemed to blossom into motherhood and our relationship, which had cooled, was reignited. We scrimped and saved, I borrowed one hundred dollars from my Mother and we bought our first car, a 1938 Plymouth coupe for two hundred.

And by this time I had moved out of the DF station and was a full-fledged air traffic controller, a tower operator in the control tower atop the main hangar. I was fast learning the trade and in fact got a chance to work as a GCA operator for several months. It was the old FPN 18 search and the SPN 16, final approach radars. There were pedals to pump to move the radar cursor. And my annual evaluations were out of sight! Life was good!

In fact, one day the squadron commander had me report to his office. It seems that there was a shortage of 2nd Lts. and, after a long conversation, he said that I had been recommended by the tower officer to go to Officers Training School. He had concurred, and I was flabbergasted! At the time, there was no college requirement and I had taken the High School GED and passed it with a high score. All I could say was to ask him, tongue tied and stammering, if I could think about it. He replied he had to have an answer in twenty-four hours.

When I got home and burst into the house, Alice was at the table feeding Mike. Excitedly I explained what had happened. She responded that she could not live by herself with Mike. I said I am sure they could live with my mom, or perhaps the Stuarts would help us. She refused and I begged and pleaded, but she had made up her mind.

The next day I went back and reported to the CO and gave him my decision. He looked at me sternly and asked if I was aware how important this decision was. I said I was aware but I could not, for personal reasons, take the assignment. He briskly dismissed me and off I went.

It was one of the biggest mistakes of my life. I remember I did not go to my part time job that night, but sat at home, in my car and pouted. But eventually, after a couple days, I forgave Alice, and pressed on.

One day, a nurse who we had gotten to know very well suddenly asked us one day if we would like to buy her house. It was a small one bedroom with a yard and no garage, flat roofed and clapboard construction. Not very nice, but she said she was leaving Illinois in a hurry and would sell it to us for nothing down and fifty two dollars per month payment for a fifteen year mortgage.

I could not believe our luck and we immediately moved into our "new" house.

Now the rush was on to furnish our new home, and every cent went for this purpose. Fortunately my cafe manager raised my pay to one dollar and gave me ten more hours per week and we were right with the world.

The Learning Curve

In April 1954. I was promoted to S.Sgt and we were fortunate to be allowed to move on base. I got lucky and sold our $12,000 house for $13,500. I insisted we put half in savings and not touch it and Alice agreed. I was finally able to quite washing dishes. Things were going well, the old car did not break that often, Mike was now walking and getting into trouble, and Alice and I started down the inevitable road of just putting up with each other.

But in June of 1954 there came another wrinkle. The Korean War had, of course ended in 1953, but there was still turmoil and strife in the country, because South Korea was still unstable. The military still had some functions, mostly of assistance and recovery. I received orders for sixty days TDY (temporary duty) with 3rd MOB at Osan, Korea, K-55. I left and Alice and Mike remained in base housing, where I had made arrangements for all of my pay to go to her. I would exist on the little TDY pay generated in those days.

Osan was one of those military oddities. Located about as hour south of Seoul, it had been built from scratch in the early 1950s outside of a town, Pyteenqtacek,(I believe I spelled it right,) referred to by the GIs as "the City." It had, I recall, a group of F-86s and a few support C-47s with a 9,000 foot runway. We were shorthanded, the normal AFCS Squadron had rotated out a few months before, and for some reason, no one came in to relieve them. So 3rd MOB was tasked. MOB, in turn requested support and our group, for whatever reason, were tasked.

We, two per shift, were working twelve hour shifts during the day and two sixes to cover the rest of the time. The midnight shift had one person. Even so, we had a chance to sneak out and go to "The City."

Like all GIs since Julius Caesar, the first order of business was a beer and then the girls. I tied up with another married S.Sgt., Joe Wilks from Des Moines Iowa, and we had a ball. We had decided that it would be cheaper if we could meet the same girl every time we got a chance, and so we hunted and were successful. The going price was three dollars for the night, we got it down to two dollars, twice a month.

In August I rotated back to the States, of course right back into base housing at Scott and my family. Unfortunately, Alice had to spend some of the savings...apparently the old car developed a wheeze and she had to have it fixed, but we still had $400, half of our original savings.

Things went along as life does, a few bumps here and there, but essentially everything was working well.

My favorite story about Mike. I had often warned him about leaving his toys out after dark. At the supper table, one night, I asked him if he had brought his ball in. He looked down and in a quivering, small voice said, "No." I told him to get up and go get his ball. He went to the door, opened it, looked outside and turned to me saying, "Dark outside." I sternly replied, "That's okay, God is out there, he will protect you." Mike turned his head and peering out the door said, "God, throw ball!" I fell off my chair!

But as it happens in the military, apparently it was to be my time in the box. In October of 1955 I received orders for remote duty transferring me to Galena Air Force Station, Alaska. We made some hurried phone calls, and I suspect Alice mended a few fences, and the Stuarts agreed to let Alice stay with them in Yermo while I was at the remote site.

So off we went in my clunker, which fortunately was being good and did not cause us any grief. I dropped my family off at the Stuarts, stayed a few days, grabbed a bus to Travis AFB and caught a flight to Ladd AFB, Fairbanks Alaska. From there I was flown via C-54 to Galena, located half way between Fairbanks and Nome.

What a place! There was a total of perhaps forty-five airman, a VFR Control Tower and was all commanded by a 2nd Lt. We had one runway, six-thousand feet, one refueling station, one mess hall ,several pieces of heavy equipment and one part weather station/base ops. There were 5 tower operators with a T.Sgt. in charge. We all lived on the second floor of an old hangar. About eight miles west, was the reason for our existence, the AC&W (aircraft control and warning) site called Campion. It was somewhat limited, but not as bad as we were. And above all, it had the first of what became known as an "all ranks club.

Twice a week, a twin engine Alaska Airlines flight would brighten our day. The surroundings were perfectly flat and oddly, in Alaska, no mountains in sight except for the one eight miles west, a solitary hill populated by the AC&W outfit. The summers were super, in the high seventies and usually no clouds in the sky.

As expected, the winter temperature got down to fifteen or so...not bad until the wind started to blow and it snowed. It you were outside it became miserable in a hurry. There was a two man rule that insisted that, during snowstorms. If you were out you had to have a buddy. Shortly, I will tell you a story of a snowstorm.

Other than the weekly movie on Saturday night in the mess hall, not much happened. There was no club to go to, no library or gym...pretty much nothing. Boredom was a killer and the longer you were there the worse it became. The pinochle games seemed to go on nonstop, intermeshed with poker, and euchre, for the few of us who could play it. Even cribbage had its devotees.

Once a week we would visit the group laundry, which had, I believe eight washers and dryers, one of which was always broke. The BX was three shelves in BaseOps, manned by the BaseOps clerk. No booze of any type was carried or, theoretically, allowed on site.

Galena village had a total population of around one hundred-fifty Inuit natives who fished the river, the Talkeetna, which bordered it on the opposite side of the base. During the winter they hunted elk and caribou, and the few wolves that got in their way. As I recall there were no more than twenty structures, most thrown together with odd pieces of lumber, but well insulated, occasionally with animal pelts. There was little vegetation to be seen, and the streets were dust in the summer and ankle deep ice and slush in the winter. A post office, bar, small school and a trading post was it.

However, in the trading post that we were prone to visit, worked a thirty-year old Indian. After five months at Galena, she started to become more beautiful every visit. I finally made up some excuse to leave the barracks, got blissfully loaded with her, and went home with her that night.

I would occasionally visit her but this affair came to a screeching halt two months later when her husband was released from prison and returned home. I stayed out of the village for the remainder of my tour.

And now my snowstorm story. Three times a week, two of us would take a jeep up to Campion to deliver their mail. One of our priorities at Galena was to always keep the road clear during the wintertime because the snow would drift two feet high on the road and block resupply to Campion. During the winter, with the Jeep and ourselves properly winterized, we would, based on winning a lottery drawing, do "the

Campion run" and of course we would always have the shopping lists of those less fortunate. For safety's sake, we were required to return to Galena by nine P.M.

On this particular February afternoon, I and another won the pool. And off we went, about four in the afternoon. It was snowing with a slight breeze but forecasted to stay moderate.

By seven P.M. I was drunk as a hoot owl and my buddy was in the same shape. I told him I was going to stay the night and for him to go back, the hell with the buddy rule. Besides the jeep had a PRC 9 radio installed, and he could call for help if need be. So he left.

And as I was told a couple days later, I swore in my drunken stupor, that he had abandoned me and I was going to find him. By now there was a slight blizzard and the conditions were beginning to get poor. So I set off on foot to Galena. Got about a mile down the road and passed out in a snowbank.

One of the guys in the Campion bar started to worry, called Galena and found I had not returned and alerted them. Two of my buddies started off immediately, and coming around a bend, spotted one leg with boot, by the side of the road. The rest of me was covered with about an inch of snow.

The guys trundled me into the track, snuck me into the barracks and piled me high with blankets, and I started to come around. I never thought I would stop shivering. The guys kept me supplied with hot coffee, and I drank a lot of it. The night passed and I considered myself fortunate that the commander had never found out.

And so it went, get up, go to chow (which was excellent), climb to the tower, be briefed, check my equipment, pull out my pocketbook and read. Maybe one inbound or two, doze off, wake up and go back to reading. Eventually relieved, off to the mess hall, back for cards and in the rack. And so it continued…

The Acceleration

In October 1956, I elected to extend my tour with duty at Ladd AFB, outside of Fairbanks, Alaska and the Air Force allowed Mike and Alice to join me.

On a chilly afternoon in early October, I met them as they got off the airplane and was I very excited. I hugged them both. Alice seemed a little heavier, but was still beautiful and managed to look like a new-lywed. Mike, age three, looked great in his new coat, with hood. I got them stashed in the old jalopy I had bought and took them to our home, a 1 bedroom house on the outskirts of Fairbanks, which I had rented 2 weeks earlier. Two days before, base housing had delivered our furniture. The rent was, like everything else in Alaska, fifty percent higher than in the States. But our subsistence allowance helped take the pressure off, but money again was very tight. And what really helped was being promoted to S.Sgt.

Ladd AFB coexisted with its Army counterpart, Fort Wainwright. It was a large base and was home not only to a F-86 Fighter Wing, but also to a Squadron of B-52s, "Cocked and Locked." The Army had a brigade there essentially to train the eskimo scout companies spread around the western edge of Alaska. And about twenty-five miles to the southeast was Eielson AFB, a SAC base with the accompanying U-2 and other classified operations. Three hundred fifty miles to the south was Anchorage, the home of Elmendorf AFB.

I was, of course, assigned to the control tower and there, except for a too brief stint, I stayed. The tower chief, M.Sgt. Carl Chappel, was an outstanding NCOIC and took great interest in his men, even to the extent of loaning us money when the occasion arose. And he was fair and firm. Carl became my role model as a NCOIC in the years to come.

Almost from the start, I started bugging him about the possibility of a TDY assignment to the FAA RAPCON, located downstairs. I reminded him that I had worked radar and I had graduated from the school.

RAPCON stands for Radar Approach Control Center. It has the responsibility of keeping all enroute aircraft, in bad weather, separated using several techniques. They were also responsible for controlling all aircraft during landing and takeoff. Most of this work was done with radar, but not all. Lateral, vertical and horizontal separation also came into play, and was often intermeshed with radar separation.

To try and grease the skids, I would go in early to work and bum around in the RAPCON, getting to know the RAPCON Chief of Operations, casually mention my experience and the school, and he would allow me to perform some administrative functions, like reloading the strip holders.

These were one by nine inch accessories that held the AF Form 1360 and 1361s. These forms were used to represent aircraft at various stages of their flight, one for departures and the other for arrivals. And on occasion they were used to control enroute aircraft. They were placed in the strip holder stacked, normally by altitude, and were to the right of the particular operators radar screen.

Eventually I got the RAPCON Chief to promise that he would accept me for ninety days and see if I could get facility rated, meaning that I would be fully qualified.

I continued my merciless harangue and Carl made the mistake of telling me that he didn't think it could be done, but if the FAA agreed, he would cut orders. I responded that they had, he grimaced and was true to his word.

About two months after Alice arrived, base housing opened up for us so in we went, along with our issued furniture.

The enlisted housing was composed of block long identical grey two story structures, each composed of six units, all units in the block either two or three bedroom. There was one block with four bedrooms homes. .We were assigned, of course, a two bedroom unit. In the parking area within the complex there were electrical outlets on posts, as there were on most military bases in severe weather areas. Not only were they in the housing area, but also spread throughout the base. These were for head bolt heaters.

Because of the severe temperatures during the winter, all vehicles in Alaska needed to have a head bolt heater. It was a simple device, a heating element installed by replacing one of the engine head bolts. Without this, when the temperature dropped below freezing, the engine block and components could fail.

Our assigned quarters were, in fact, the nicest house we had lived in so far. A small kitchen, and a small dining room off of the kitchen, with the living room and fireplace adjoining. Upstairs was the bath and two bedrooms. Like most military families, our neighbors were kind and helpful. The day we moved in several came over and offered to help, one even bringing a hot lunch.

Nice, in fact one across the street was too nice. Several months after we had moved in, one evening while Alice was gone with a friend to a movie, this girl showed up at the backdoor asking for the proverbial "cup of sugar." I supplied it and a romp on the living room floor. I guess I flunked the course because she never came back.

Not long after, Steve, our second son, arrived. He was quiet and a little reserved, even from birth, and would stare off in space. It was hard to get a giggle out of him for he was reticent, so we visited the doctor who examined Steve and announced that he was perfectly normal, just "preoccupied." Mike, at three, was rapidly developing a selfish and demanding attitude and took up a great deal of Alice's time, and I might add, patience. But she found time to join the NCO Wives Club and the AACS Wives Club and was normally busy doing her own thing.

Two weeks later I walked into RAPCON and was assigned to the swing shift, four P.M. to midnight. I was to spend the first thirty days learning the equipment, area, rules and regulations and pass the first two parts of the qualification tests. It was no easy matter. Their area was the whole of Alaska beginning in the south, halfway to Anchorage. But luckily I had learned the area when I was rated for the tower, but it was still hard. I spent many nights at home, burning the midnight oil.

And I passed on my first try. And now I was assigned to floor duty.

I started off in the enroute position, which was controlling aircraft on and off the airways with the use of slips of paper. The 1360 and 1361s. The term "airways" was a descriptive term. It meant that an aircraft would tune in a radio beacon and fly to it, tune in another further along and fly to it, etc. until they got to their destination, in our case, within forty miles of Ladd, or in some cases another location. They would then be "handed off" to a terminal controller who would issue instructions to position the aircraft at a specific altitude, ten miles from the airport, on a required heading where they would be "handed over" to a final controller, ten miles from touchdown. The final controller would issue headings and recommend altitude changes all the way to the runway. And coincidentally, we would be generating departures through the same airspace.

It was fast, quick paced, and highly stressful. My cup of tea!

I was then assigned to the terminal position and fell in love. It seemed that I was mentally suited for this challenge, and every operation was just that, a challenge. I would, before taking the position, stand behind the operator and study the strips to become familiar with the traffic, next I did the same thing with the scheduled departures.

I let my mind open up, and I could, in fact, visualize the whole area and the positions of the aircraft and could almost feel it expand. That was the mental setup that continued as I worked the position. In my mind I could see the traffic positions change and the modifications I needed came almost automatically. You normally were controlling ten to fifteen aircraft simultaneously and at the same time working the departures up to enroute control. Occasionally there was a departure controller, but only during the busiest periods. I absolutely loved this position!!

If you stood back and took in the whole operation, and were knowledgeable, it would seem like a ballet, each movement and command in unison with someone across the room, part of the mass yet totally separate. It was fascinating to watch and exhilarating to do; my ninety days passed too soon and I left RAPCON with sadness and a letter of commendation from the FAA Regional HQ in Anchorage, Alaska.

I was the only Ladd AFB Tower Operator dual qualified.

Money was short, so I began looking for a part time job in Fairbanks and almost immediately I found one. I applied for and was hired to sell hot dogs at the stock car races. So on the Saturdays and Sundays I did not work for Carl Chappel, I flogged my hotdogs, rain or shine. The track was used for stock car races in the summer months and dog sled races in the winter and the grandstands, which held about 3,000, were always filled. And so I wandered throughout the stands, barking my "dogs," and being thankful when anyone ordered.

The summer days were bright with a slight breeze, and the skies cloudless.

The second Saturday that I worked, in August, the announcer stated," And here they come again folks, those daredevil parachute jumpers, off to your right." I stopped dead and focused on a small plane approaching from the north at, I estimated, 1,000 feet. Out popped two objects who fell and then opened their parachutes, both landing on the inside of the track. The crowd were on their feet, clapping and cheering. The two parachutists then wandered thru the crowd with a long white bag apparently collecting money.

I was hooked! I decided that this was something I had to do!

At home that evening, I explained what had transpired and Alice gleefully said to "go for it," but only if she could watch. I hugged her and she patted me on my ass and so, the next weekend, I contacted one of the jumpers.

He was tall slim, balding, late thirties, in an orange jump suit and jump boots. On his left breast was a patch in the shape of Alaska that read "Fairbanks Parachute Club." With a wide engaging smile, he introduced himself as Bob Sinclair. I explained that I wanted to try it and he invited me down to Tommy's Elbow Room that evening about seven, and we would talk about it.

I went home and excitedly told Alice what had occurred and asked her again she thought. She said it would be a neat thing to try and repeated that maybe she could come out and watch?

I nodded my head, did the dishes and helped her change the sheets on the beds. I started to get the vacuum sweeper out, and she stopped me saying kindly, "You've earned your kitchen pass, go for it." So at seven P.M. sharp I walked through the doors of Tommy's Elbow Room.

Bob Sinclair, Parachutist

Tommy's had been in Fairbanks for years, and to the best of my knowledge it is still there, on Second Street, and still run by Tommy Paskvan. The bar ran down the left side and there were tables and a small dance floor on the right. It was always dimly lit, even during the day.

There was Bob and a few others sitting at the bar, all talking at the same time. He recognized me and motioned me over. Introductions were in order, Lyle Kneff, Jim Songger, Frank Scroggins, and Marilyn Board, Bob's girlfriend. They were a loud, raucous and extroverted group, poking fun at each other and joking about each other's sexual prowess, ability and dimensions. The favorite drink was beer, and I soon learned about Flaming Mammie's.

Lyle, in his late teens, today had made his third jump and as a result, was to drink a Flaming Mammie. For each of the first five jumps, members of the Club were tasked to do so. It was a shot glass of Vodka, on fire. The group would count from one to five, and at five the novice would quickly tip his head back and swallow, hoping he would not spill any on his chest. In point of fact, when it was a female, we would all gather close hoping she did spill it on her chest so we could put it out. Wouldn't want her to get burnt, would we?

And Bob began jump school. He explained that the dues for the club were twenty-five dollars a month and that we would be charged off the aircraft tach for the flying time. Any collections we made from the crowd would go to defray the cost of the airplane. The club initially provided the parachutes, but you were expected to come up with your own.

He announced, "You and the jumpmaster, after he checks you out, will board the 'puddle jumper', and you'll sit in the doorway," he continued with a grin, "when the jumpmaster thinks you are about one minute from exit, he'll hold up, naturally, his middle finger. When you arrive over the release point, the Jumpmaster will tap you out." He added, somewhat wolfishly, "You will immediately spread your arms and legs wide, look down at your ripcord handle and pull all of the way out, If the main doesn't open, look at the reserve ripcord handle and pull it all of the way out. Reach up and grab the risers, bend your knees, toes pointed down, and land. Get on your feet and collect your canopy, that's all there is to it." He grinned broadly and punched me on the shoulder. "Time for you to buy a round," he said.

The next Thursday, at Lyle's house, I donned the rig for the first time, Bob explaining the various parts and how they worked. He then showed me the proper way to land and had me do a few PLFs (parachute landing falls). That was the end of jump school. We three then settled down to drink a beer.

The airport was a three thousand foot dirt strip, orientated north-south with the race track being four miles west. We therefore, would takeoff, make two turns lining up as appropriate and leave the airplane over the track.

We were concerned about the cost of the flying time, so the jump was done quickly with no fanfare, and at low altitudes, most of the time about eight hundred feet. Sometimes, depending on the weather, lower.

Saturday, the big day arrived. Alice had arranged for a babysitter so she was there to watch. Bob introduced her to the other 'watchers,' wives and girlfriends. Bob looked at the sky and said, "All right… about six knots from the north." We jumped in my car and at the airport, by the side of the little yellow Cessna 150, I nervously donned the rig. Bob then had me do a PLF with the rig on. I did it wrong and he had me repeat it. With his infectious grin, he asked me if I understood what to do and if I had enough money to buy a round at Tommy's, I smiled to show no fear, and he and I boarded the Cessna, right door removed. Bob had a big smile on his face and kept up the conversation.

We took off to the north and the little airplane made the first left turn. I lost track of the ground. As we straightened out I swear the tree tops were within reach, the wind was howling in my face but not enough to absorb the perspiration. We made the second turn and the aircraft pitched and bumped a little. Christ, we were really low!

Bob waved at me sitting in the door, the wind blast was fierce and the little airplane rocked constantly. Looking down I could swear I could reach out and touch the bottoms of the trees. Bob leering, gave me the finger. I was scared shitless! We were over the track, Bob grinned and tapped me hollering, "See ya at Tommy's" and out I went, and he followed.

I pivoted on my left foot and pushed off spreading my arms and legs, caught a glimpse of the racetrack, looked down at the ripcord handle and pulled, just that fast. A jolt, I checked my canopy to make sure it was well, and looked down. The view was just great but I did not have enough time to find Alice in the Grandstands

The ground came up in a hurry, I impacted and rolled over, getting to my feet and…I was exhilarated! It was the most stupefying thing I had ever done! As was getting out of the harness, Lyle and another showed up and helped me. I hugged them both! And here came Bob and Alice, they got hugs, also.

I immediately wanted to do it again, but reality set in when Bob told me what my share of the tach time was. He gave me my pilot chute, and we worked the crowds for about an hour and at the days end, had collected over $400; $200 for the aircraft left and $200 for Tommy's!

At Tommy's, they chanted, "One two three four five," and down it went! And a lot more after. I had passed their test!

And Bob told me a little about himself. He came from Michigan, joined the Army at eighteen and went thru jump school being assigned to the 101st Airborne Division. He served three years and upon discharge, decided to go to Pt. Barrow, Alaska and work in the oil fields there. Upon arrival, he talked his boss into letting him be a crane operator, which he had never done. The work dried up after a year and Bob went to Nome and began hard hat diving for a salvage company. Again, something he had never done but talked his way in. He said he made a couple dives but did not like it.

In 1950, he came to Fairbanks and did odd jobs, mostly working in a warehouse or supply depot and started the Fairbanks Parachute Club.

Ladd AFB, like all military installations, had a salvage yard where equipment broken or too old was stored, put up for sale or destroyed. One of the items were B-8 canopies and harnesses, which if seven years old, were withdrawn from use. Here Bob bought his first rig.

He had no reserve parachute, in fact made his first six jumps without one. With this surplus canopy he started to make parachute jumps locally and in Palmer, outside Anchorage.

As the club grew so did the equipment problem. Bob found, at salvage, an old Model 9710 heavy duty sewing machine. Based on a design invented by Frank Derry, a Smokejumper rigger, Bob modified his canopy with" Slots and Tails" and slip risers, which made the canopy some-what steerable. He also located some C-7 chest packs at Elmendorf AFB in Anchorage, and purchased these for ten dollars each.

The club had solved its equipment problems and towards the end of 1954, there were about twelve jumpers in the club, and most evenings were taken up modifying the rigs interspersed with several visits to Tommy's. And by the way, helmets or goggles were not worn, until we started to do three or four second delays. And in 1954, the club had its only fatality.

They were jumping at Creamer's Dairy, a farm on the outskirts of Fairbanks. Aboard the second lift of the day was an Army Sgt. who was making his second jump. He exited, momentarily assumed the prone position, came in and pulled. His canopy did not inflate, at all, being what we referred to as a "streamer." He never deployed his reserve and impacted on a wooden fence. Bob said that they never determined why the main did not inflate or why he did not go for his reserve.

Every Saturday and Sunday, weather permitting summer and winter, we would jump at the racetrack or at Creamer's Dairy grazing field. Occasionally we would journey to Palmer, Nome, Talkeetna, and Livengood and other places to jump, but up to this point never out of the territory. And a story about Bob's adventures.

One summer, I believe in 1952, at an airshow in Palmer, Bob was to ride the top wing of an old Stearman bi-plane, and at the top of the third loop, hopefully at 3,000 feet, drop off, freefall to 800 and open, landing in front of the crowds.

The top of the loop was reached and Bob let go. Unfortunately the pilot had miscounted because rather than banking away, completed the loop and the prop,, cut every suspension line four feet above Bob's head. He got his reserve out at tree top level and impacted in a scrub forest. As soon as it was possible, he went looking for the pilot, who was nowhere to be found. This story was published in several periodicals of the day, including Parachutist Magazine.

In 1957 Bob and Marilyn were married, I being the best man. They had a small house on the outskirts of the city, and both were employed, Bob as a warehouseman, Marilyn at a bank. And on weekends Bob would jump and Marilyn would watch from the ground. Finally Marilyn decided to try it and Bob jumpmastered her, all going well. I in fact, spotted her on her third jump. She froze and I had to 'nudge' her out. It was the last jump she made. Unfortunately their marriage did not work and they were divorced a year later.

Bob, at this point was unemployed so he stayed with us on base snuggled up in a sleeping bag in our front room, for almost six months. In May of 1959, Bob and I traveled south to Palmer Alaska to make a few jumps during a airshow.

This gig was different because we had signed a contract to perform and were being paid $200 per jump with the aircraft, our old standby, a Cessna 170, being provided free of charge. And so we did the dastardly deed making two each from 3,000 feet, one for the morning show and one in the afternoon. When we finished, Bob said to me, with a twinkle in his eye, "Come on, lets stash our shit. I got someone I want you to meet."

So we grabbed a cab and traveled up the hills to a beautiful home on the bluffs overlooking Anchorage. Bob knocked on the door and a lady in her fifties responded, throwing her arms around Bob and saying, "What a surprise, come in, Lowell is in the den with someone you will enjoy meeting." Bob just grinned and motioned me in. Lowell who? With that we went through the dining room being joined by a slightly built fifty-year-old or so man who stuck his hand out to me and said, "Hi, I'm Lowell Thomas Jr, how do you do?"

I was stunned. I knew of Mr. Thomas, as did everyone in Alaska! He put his arm around Bob's shoulder and ushered us into the den.

There sat a burly man with grey hair and beard, wearing a checkered lumberjack jacket. On the low table in front of him stood a bottle of scotch. I glanced at him…this cannot be!

Ernest Hemmingway stood and held out his hand and I tentatively shook it. His blue eyes twinkling. The 1954 winner of the Nobel Prize and me in the same room! I glanced at Bob and he was thunderstruck! And they were actually talking to me! Lowell Thomas and Ernest Hemingway! Mr. Thomas told us to make ourselves at home, and I stumbled to a seat across the table from the author! Jesus Christ I was beside myself! In reply to his question about where I came from, I quickly, and nervously commented that I came from the same area in Illinois that he did, Oak Park. He nodded and made a few comments about Chicago. I shook my head, still speechless.

Mr. Thomas asked what Bob had been up to and what was he doing so far south. Bob explained about the airshow, and they entered a 'catch up' conversation. I just stupidly looked on, covertly glancing at Mr. Hemmingway. I could not believe my eyes!

Mr. Hemmingway asked a few questions about parachuting and the three of them picked up the conversation. I think I ventured forth a couple times, but in essence sat there with my mouth wired shut.

Bob, amused, said that he had brought a short story about low level parachuting that I had written and asked if they would like to see it. I protested but like always, Bob would not listen. Bob handed it to Mr. Thomas who put his glasses on, scanned it and smilingly, handed it to Mr. Hemmingway. He took a moment and read the short article. He looked and me, grinned and said, "That's good, in my contemporary style, ya gonna publish it?" I stammered and said I didn't know.

It eventually was published in 1964. Bob and I sat for the rest of the night into the wee hours of the morning listening to the two of them talk. I still was dumfounded, and even Bob, as much of an extrovert that he was, had little to say. They talked of Europe, what it was in the twenties and thirties and, what it had become, forecasting a common European currency and addressing the current political stance of some of the notorious people in Washington DC, most of them friends in common.

Mr. Hemmingway revisited his "The Sun Also Rises" and "The Old Man and The Sea," also making some comments about his two sons and one daughter. Mr. Thomas, who was well traveled, recalled things far away and exotic spots, An adventurer in his own right, he drew comparisons between himself and his father, a noted commentator during World War Two.

I prayed that a tape recorder would suddenly appear.

They spoke of Ansel Adams, Tennessee Williams, Harry Truman and his MacArthur fiasco, Charles Drew and Mr. Hemmingway's dalliances with Betty Grable, Lauren Bacall and a few others. A second bottle of scotch arrived and was consumed. They continued to talk, with Bob adding a few observations. Once I even gave an opinion, over the MacArthur affair. As the sun was rising there was a lull, and Bob called us a cab.

On the way back to Palmer, Bob explained that he had met Mr. Thomas when he had arrived in Nome to report on an oil rig problem. He swore he did not know that there would be a guest. Mr. Thomas went on to become the Lt. Governor of Alaska, Mr. Hemmingway tragically committed suicide a few years later.

For the rest of my tour, I continued to jump with the club, once going to Vancouver, British Columbia for the first ever competition, at which I failed miserably, but met Loy Brydon, Jacque Istel and several other movers and shakers.

Occasionally Bob would rent a Cessna 150 or Piper and we would fly to Livengood or Hitachnia for lunch. It was not until we got off the ground the first time that Bob admitted that he had no pilot's license. I asked him how he was able to rent a plane, and with his best Sinclair smirk, he replied, "the manager used to be in the 101st Abn."

And about this time Parachutist magazine had formed a quasi-official licensing board, and who was now recognized as the Founding Father and began issuing licenses, A thru D, with D requiring the most jumps. We had never kept track, so we guessed a lot and the whole club applied.

Bob and two others who had kept good records were approved. The rest including mine, were declined for lack of proof. I believe Bobs was D86 or something like that. Eventually I guess this got to be a big thing, but it did not hamper me.

A couple years after Alice and I left Alaska, in Dec of 1959, Bob came south, settled in the Los Angeles area and formed, with two friends, Paraventures, a company that did stunt jumping for the movies, notably the series "Ripcord," and taught various TV personalities how to jump.

In addition they did work for Pepsi, Coke, some food chains and various other advertisers. Bob in fact, is recognized as the originator of helmet mounted cameras and produced excellent air to air photography. Viewing his work, you would swear that the camera was mounted on something solid and unwavering. Bob and I corresponded for several years and then the letters stopped.

In their spare time they were teaching parachuting at Lake Elsinore and two other locations. But when the national interest in parachuting dried up, so did the residuals and fees. Paraventures declared bankruptcy and Bob went to Arizona to open another Club.

Then one day I got a call from him. He was in town visiting another friend, an ex-smokejumper named Jim Pearson, who with Lyle Hoffman in 1958, had made the first baton pass in Vancouver. Jan and I drove over and there he was. He had grown a little around the middle and less on his head. But the thing that struck me the most was his attitude and demeanor. No longer the brash extrovert, with a ready smile and punch to the shoulder. He was quiet and withdrawn, almost pensive in his conversation. In reply to my many questions, the answers were short and curt. I don't think he smiled more than a couple times.

I learned, from our mutual friend, that life had not been kind to him and that he had been reduced to living out of his van and spent his time traveling from one friend to another, still occasionally making a jump. His only income was a Social Security Check. At one point all of us piled into my car and went down to the drop zone at Davis, right behind the University.

When the young jumpers found out who was in their midst, we were swamped with everyone wanting Bob and Jim to sign their log books.

That night we brought Bob home for supper and offered our guest room but he insisted on staying in his van. During the night I snuck over and placed three $100 bills under his wiper. The next morning I found them on my screen door. His few letters were as painful to read as it must have been to write. He admitted to being in financial difficulty and he said he had come to grips with what his life had become in comparison to what it once was. But the rest of the letter seemed upbeat and positive, he signed the letter "PULL," as he always had.

I offered to pay his expenses if he would come to Sacramento, and provide him room and board at no charge and received no response. And his letters slowed and were more and more pensive and full of retrospect.

Bob died in Florida in 2014.

Years before, he had been enshrined in the Parachutist Hall of Fame and rightly so. He was the most alive and influential man I have ever met. I still miss him.

Meanwhile, Back Home

When I got back from the initiation at Tommy's at about two in the morning, Alice was furious. Mike had broken a dish and as I walked into the house I could hear Steve wailing. She insisted that never again would I stay out late, and the fighting started. Eventually we ignored each other and off to bed we went,

The next morning I apologized and told her that if it happened again, I wanted her with me. She said, happily, that she could always arrange a babysitter, in fact, the girl across the street had already volunteered!

At that I went to work.

I had a habit of going to the gym as often as I could, and today the Sgt. in charge mentioned that a civilian on base, who was some kind of judo guy, had asked if he could teach judo classes. Because of the current SAC emphasis on judo training, he had agreed and had posted a sign-up sheet. It was free, except for the uniform. Needless to say, I had always been interested in personnel combat, so I signed up.

Classes were Monday, Wednesday and Friday at six P.M. At the first class, Sensi (teacher) Tarmar gave us our orientation. There were about ten students. He was a Sandan, or third degree black belt and had been studying Kodokwan judo for about twelve years, three of it in Japan. Classes would be two hours long and the only other dojo (school) was at Eielson AFB Base so that would be the only club we would contest with. He would order the gis (uniforms) tonight and should have them by the first class, next Monday. We got to our feet and he gave the first lesson, how to bow. Class dismissed!

For the rest of the time I was stationed at Ladd, three times a week, I would go to the gym and get beat up, and give a few beatings as well. Eventually we had about twenty-five people in our class, including two ladies, one of whom, a Captain's wife, I hit on.

Not only did she turn me down, she wrote a letter to my squadron commander.

When we met, he was not pleased at all. He apparently knew the Capt. and his wife so he phrased "in no uncertain terms would I ever" and "at no time while I was in his command." I got the message.

Several months later, I went to a Parachute Club meeting. It adjourned to Tommy's, I got drunk and wandered home about one A.M. Alice was in her furious mode which continued into the next day. At supper that night, as she was preparing pork chops, things got out of hand and in frustration and anger, she threw a frozen pork chop at me which missed my head by inches and imbedded in the wall.

The next day base housing maintenance arrived to patch the hole and fell down laughing while I made the report. I was charged fifty-two dollars for the repair, which I had to borrow from Sgt. Chappell, even though I was still flogging my hot dogs occasionally at the Track. One of the guys in the Parachute Club was an Army SFC named Skip Minnix. He and I became friends and it remained so over the years, Skip was an ex-Special Forces trooper and asked if I would like to join his class, and I said, "Hell yes." And so, spasmodically, over the next two months I learned to ski with the Army Scout Company. And loved it.

At this point Bob lost his job and moved in with us, in a sleeping bag on the floor. It was crowded, but Bob spent most of his time looking for work or at the club house. Eventually he found a job and moved in with his new girlfriend, Shelia Robs who was in real estate and was doing very well. We would often kid Shelia about falling out of an airplane but she always declined.

My life and career as a control tower operator continued uneventfully until one day, while I was working...

The command post's phone rang, which always precluded a problem of some magnitude.

DEFCON 2, was called. This was a state of national readiness defined as a possible strategic situation that could lead to an immediate nuclear attack.

They advised that AC&W had picked up two Russian Bison Bombers 26,000 feet inbound 132 degrees, our airspace penetration time twenty-three minutes, 138 miles northwest Of Kotzebue.420 knots. Translated, if they continued course and airspeed, they would be over me in less than an hour.

We were placed on a real alert! It was the late fifties and tensions with Russia were high. The sirens blew and everyone scuttled for cover!

Most of the military had been briefed that the possibility of a Russian "incursion" was probable and what we and our families were to do in the event one occurred. There had been several practice ones, which everyone had ignored. But this was real!

The F-86s came roaring out of their revetment and launched, six aircraft, as I recall. We were frantically trying to get everyone out of the proposed combat airspace, and land everyone we could at other airfields. Which did not have reflex fighters.

All air traffic in the Alaskan Area came to a screeching halt. I never heard what happened, but after about forty-five minutes, the DEFCON status changed to all clear and the operation started to recover.

A couple hours later I got home and found my neighborhood still unsettled about the experience. Alice and the boys were ok, but one of our neighbors was still upset and crying, so Alice went over to help her calm down. The possibility of DEFCON 2 had been scoffed at by many, and now the brutal political situation started to sink in. I remember for several days later there were calls of alarm and concern posted in the Fairbanks paper. People had been rudely awoken.

My time was spent doing parachuting stuff, at the gym or flogging the dogs and spending time with the family. Mike and Steve, of course, were growing, still at home, and Mike was getting more rambunctious than ever. He had pushed a neighbor girl off her bicycle which caused some problems. Luckily, In September he would start kindergarten which would give Alice a break.

She and I were getting along well. I had talked her into joining the judo dojo and she was in a female class that met right after ours. The Captain's wife had dropped out. And Alice had found a neighbor that was willing to babysit, for almost nothing (not the girl across the street!) She was also busy with the NCO Wives Club and was expanding her social life. Time went slowly by.

Finally, in March of 1959, after several matches, most of which I won, I was awarded Ichi-dan, or first degree black belt. It was a major event and was attended by some from the Parachute Club, those at work including Carl Chappel, and other friends. And I got wind of a judo teaching possibility. A small gym in downtown Fairbanks was trying to expand its customer base and had decided on offering something extra. I called them, went down to the gym and discussed the possibilities. Fortunately they had a twenty by twenty mat. They also had two body bags and one speed bag. I would teach three times a week for two hours, charge fifty dollars per student per month, twenty-five of which would go to the owners and we would begin instruction in thirty days.

I could see the possibility of saying bye-bye to the hot dog business. So I quit the on base dojo, put an ad in the local Fairbanks newspaper and nervously waited for any response. In the meantime, I began giving private lessons to the owner and his wife, a short well-built black-haired flirt, about forty or so. And the second week we operated, the owner's wife and I started an affair that lasted intermittently, until I shipped out.

Towards the end of April, the owners and I did some tabulations and found we had 18 prospective students. I did some quick figuring, twenty-five dollars times eighteen= $450! I quit the hot dog business.

The first of May we opened the judo school and I had fifteen students report in. One of these, Dan Howard was an Alaska Highway Patrol Officer an ik'ku or first degree Brown belt and had come down out of curiosity. Dan was knowledgeable and an excellent teacher, and when I was reassigned in October, he took over, perhaps also with the boss's wife, I don't know.

I continued to jump but had to cut way back, having accumulated about eighty free falls. My week had gotten too full and I was spread way to thin. And at the end of July my orders arrived. I was assigned to Holloman AFB, New Mexico.

In August the club tossed me a going away party at Tommy's of course. Alice glided in on my arm, the place was packed, the three piece band overwhelmed, and Bob got up and belted a few out to everyone's surprise, not bad, kinda Tony Bennett. A fight started in the men's room but was quickly extinguished. Alice got quite drunk and when we got home, was a complete tiger in bed.

And so it continued. And in October, we said some sad goodbyes, promises to write, turned in our furniture, packed up, gave the old clunker to an Air force friend, and hit it. We were flown to McChord

AFB in Tacoma, Washington, I put the family in transit quarters, shopped around and bought a 1957 Mercury Station wagon for $300 down and eighty-six dollars a month for twenty-four months, loaded them up and off we went to our new station.

Upon arrival at Holloman, we hit it lucky and were able to move directly on base, in to what was then called Wherry Housing. They were a conglomeration of duplexes, painted white with red roof tile, in the Spanish style. The ones in our area were all three bedroom with a large fenced back yard. We only stayed four days in the guest quarters. Housing supply was amazingly efficient, once the commissary run was complete and everyone settled in, I checked into the unit.

I was, of course assigned as shift supervisor in the control tower, the tower chief being John Malloy, a short feisty Irishman with blue eyes and red hair. He had been there for about three years and loved the desert and the isolation. He took me up to the tower, showed me around and I was to report for facility training the next day. All went well and I started my career at Holloman.

In the 50s and the 60s Judo, was immensely popular even at non-SAC Bases, since SAC had made it mandatory for its aircrews. The first month I was there, I checked with the base gym and found that there was no room to teach there. However, Special Services helped me find an unused building and assigned it to the gym, for use as a dojo. I could not believe my luck.

It had a main room thirty by fifty, bathroom and showers. No heat or air but I didn't care. We were able to obtain two body bags, one speed bag and some weights from another AF gym and our gym let us have a twenty by twenty mat they had in storage.

In February 1960, I established the Holloman AFB Judo Dojo with three students. We constantly trained grappling, take downs, and chokes. I snarled, screamed begged, cajoled! I Had my foot so far up their ass I thought my knee would break! After six months we had grown to nine students and I thought we were ready. Our first match was with the Alamogordo Dojo, we won three and lost one. We slept in my station wagon or in sleeping bags to defray expenses, and normally only competed with local clubs, In 1961 I finally convinced finance to fund us. We then spread out our wings, competing with dojos in EI Paso and in Albuquerque. Generally we did well, winning more that we lost.

As a result of our record with local dojos, I petitioned the base commander for TDY funding and as a result, we participated in the All AF Judo Tournament at the AF Academy, March 1961, their team being the host. We were all inexperienced and the competition was populated by standouts, like George Harris, heavyweight, three time AAU champ, who ran the gym at Travis.

One of our judoka took second in his class, I won one and lost two. And was very pleased with the team's performance. One of the guys went on to be a Roku Dan (sixth degree) and was on the USA Judo Team.

I worked in the **VFR** Control Tower as Shift Supervisor and had A1C Ernie Passey on my crew. He was quiet and somewhat withdrawn.

The normal traffic count in military towers was about 200 per day, we consistently ran 300 or more. The reason was that we were a research and development site which not only had numerous visitors, we also had multitudes of test flights generated daily.

There were four runways, laid out in a 'X' with a set of parallels north and south.

Us common, everyday, run of the mill controllers would only use three at a time. Not Ernie, he constantly used all four. He would control the traffic for ten minutes, glance down and make a mark, look up and talk to several more, make a mark, on and on. He was doing crossword puzzles! Neither the tower chief nor I would want to change him. I have never seen a guy with that kind of concentration. And when quizzed, he could recite the location of all traffic in the pattern for the last half-hour! Unbelievable!

In the meantime, money, as always was short, but this time just a little short. I checked around and found a job as a waiter in the NCO Club, two nights a week plus weekends depending on my tower schedule. And so I put on my bow tie, grabbed my tray and set off to make the big bucks. It was a good job, boring and of course, with the dojo and the waitering, there was little time for the family. And I regretted it, but there was little to be done. Alice, to her credit, understood and supported me. It was one of the few times that she did.

And of course, eventually it happened. A T.Sgt. worked at a remote site four days a week and had knockout women. Thursday nights were bingo nights and they would show up and I got to know them reasonably well. The dojo was right next to the swimming pool which was open, during the summer, eighteen hours a day. One day as we were finishing up, the wife appeared and she was something else! I could not help but stare, and she smiled at me, and swished to my side of the pool, stretched out on a chaise lounge and yawned.

Next Thursday night she showed up by herself, I made a few moves, she batted her eyes and after I got off shift, I stopped by her house and bombs went off.

The next night at the club she and her husband showed up and one of the bartenders noticed me eying her. He leaned over and said, "Careful, you ain't the only one, she's been through the staff." That dulled my interest and from then on I came straight home.

Life continued, the boys getting bigger and bolder. And Alice found out she was pregnant, not only pregnant but pregnant with twins.

One day, at work, I got a call from the Air Police asking me to come home immediately. I called John Malloy, he hotfooted it up to the tower and I scurried for home. As I turned into my street I saw two Air Police vehicles in front of my house.

Opening the front door, here were four Air Policeman standing in front of Alice, seated on the couch, crying, and shaking. I asked the S.Sgt. "What the hell is going on?" He asked me to step outside, which we did. Turning to me he said they had a complaint from a neighbor that Alice had come over, broke into her house and assaulted her. When they questioned Alice, she said, "Damn right and I'd do it again." The Air Police then went next door to get the other side of the story. And this is what they pieced together.

Alice said that Mike and the boy next door, who were fine buddies played together often. On this day, they decided to go into the neighbor's kitchen to get a cookie. While there, the other boy went to the bathroom leaving Mike alone with the cookie jar. The mother came into the kitchen saw Mike, became upset, slapped him and physically threw him out her door, accusing him of breaking into her house to steal cookies. Mike came into our bedroom crying and told Alice what had happened. Alice got mad, went next door and punched the lady, who then called the Air Police.

About this time, the neighbor's husband showed up. He, I, and the S.Sgt. Air Police got our heads together to see if we could come up with a solution that would not require that neither the ladies would be cited. Eventually we decided, that both ladies needed to be warned to stay away from each other until everyone became rational. Both I and the other husband agreed and we went off to brief our respective wives.

A month later I received orders assigning me to Itazuke, Japan, unaccompanied, until I could find housing. So, we packed up, I took Alice and the boys to my mom's house where she was to be cared for at the Naval Hospital, down the road, and set off for the rising sun.

Pats on The Head

Off to Itazuke AFB Japan. June 1961. Because Alice was pregnant with twins and set to deliver momentarily, she stayed behind with my mom and I went to Japan alone. I was quartered on the Kasugabaru side, a support facility that housed the troops and the headquarters element. The airport was a facility about 6 miles away. Both entities combined were referred to as Itazuke Air Force Base. You either drove or took a shuttle bus back and forth. I, having no transport yet, rode the bus.

Kasugabaru, referred to as 'K Bar' was a hotbed of bars, tiny restaurants and small hotels. There were no end of bar girls, or working girls, there being only a grammatical difference between the two. All of us in the barracks spent as much time in K Bar as we could afford. Because most of my money was going to Alice, my participation, although formidable, was infrequent. Besides, I was frantically trying to save up enough to buy us a car.

And on the twentieth of August 1961, the twins, Donald and David, were delivered in a Navy hospital close to Mom's home. Alice had sent me a telegram and I fired back that I would have enough money saved to buy a car and alert me to her arrival date. She did so, I arraigned for housing, and over they came. I was glad to see them all.

I was assigned duty in the Enroute/RAPCON Control Center. We were responsible for a 200 mile radius which contained three JASDF (Japanese Self Defense Force) bases: Ashiyas , Kumimoto and Sasebo. Sixty-percent of all traffic bound for SE Asia came through us. This RAPCON represented the best air traffic control facility I had ever worked in.

I worked with a JASDF Lt. who was a Goju karate student in Fukuoka, the nearest city, and he took me down to the dojo one night. I met the sensei, Yasakuda., rokudan (sixth degree). He stated, to join, I must do fifty pushups, fifty sit-ups and run a mile on the path in the park surrounding the dojo, and that he liked Camel cigarettes. I said "get it on" and we did. But he neglected to mention the run was on a gravel path barefooted. Luckily because of the judo, my feet were in good shape, but I still limped for months. Sensei said I needed to love pain.

For those of you who may be buffs, Sensei was a disciple of Matsutasa Oyama, a Korean immigrant who was famous for killing bulls in the Tokyo arena barehanded. In the 50s he had an unmatched reputation and most other karatekas were afraid of him. His training methods were, even for karate students, extreme. He would stand under almost freezing waterfalls for hours at a time, soak his hands in brine to toughen them and allow his students to strike him anywhere they wished.

The practice was tough and exact, and so were the matches. One evening a black belt was outside teaching a student how to do "shuto", the edge of the hand strike, and the student was attacking a two by four buried in the ground. I happened to be by the window. Sensi got in the black belts face in a rage, shouted something at him whirled and struck the board so hard it snapped off at the base. Apparently the black belt had earned his displeasure.

In most karate schools, full contact is not allowed. Points are scored for blows that might have landed. But not in Goju. There were always injuries, mostly minor, for the matches were full contact. And the various kicking techniques often brought considerable pain and embarrassment. At one point I saw one of my partners get kicked so hard he actually defecated on the mat and passed out. I loved the katas (matches) and for some reason, I did well.

As part of the katas, there was always a demonstration at the beginning. I, being the only gugakugiin (foreigner), was the star. We had one female, maybe five foot, ninety pounds, a Nidan (second degree). Yes, in broken Japanese I hit on her but she firmly rebuffed me, politely. She would approach the mat, bow to the referee and the crowd. I would assume an attack stance. And the referee would place a matchbox on my head, she would come on, get set, jump up and with the edge of her foot and knock the matchbox off, technically defeating me. The crowd were on their feet, clapping and cheering! They loved it!

Before I left Itazuke, I was awarded Shodan, first degree black belt. I think it was the first time in this dojo that a foreigner had been so honored. I think the carton of Camels once a week did it!

I had saved enough money to buy a car from a GI that was rotating home, which was the only car buying source. Other than old, I don't today recall the make. Along with buying a car I had also applied for base housing, which at Itazuke could easily mean 'living off the economy' or translated, living in a house in the Japanese community that was leased by the government. This came to pass two weeks before Alice arrived and the units were all pre-furnished so that was not a concern.

It was not much of a house, three bedroom, in the Shiashibaru district half way between the headquarters containment and the airport, in the Japanese style, poorly constructed with small rooms and had almost no insulation. Spaces which later I caulked, were visible at the top and bottom of the windows and doors. But it was home.

It was obvious that Alice needed help with four boys, so we hired a 'mama-san,' who would come in, help with the housework and care for the kids. We were extremely fortunate because we found one across the street, a short thin older lady in her sixties with grey hair tight behind her head, and a long kimono. And she agreed to work for twenty-five cents an hour! As most Japanese are, she was extremely courteous and formal in the beginning. But as time progressed she became less rigid and fit right into the family. She was looked upon by all of us as a grandmother and got the respect that she deserved and Mike was finally off to first grade.

Alice got close to our next door neighbor, Cindy Monihan whose husband, Ed, was a OSI Agent and gone a lot. Quite often, Cindy and Alice spent their days bumming around and shopping at an international ginza a few blocks from us.

And I had my only dealings with a Japanese doctor.

Alice and I had decided that four boys were enough so I went down to K Bar and found a Doctor that would perform a vasectomy. At the appointed time, I arrived and was laid, fully clothed, on a table. Looking around I could see that the equipment that he had was old and some, like his sterilizer, I recognized from my trip to Dr. Smith's office in Gurnee.

He unbuckled my pants and pulled them and my shorts to my knees. He disappeared and I had time to reflect. This was certainly much more basic than I expected. No nurse, no assistant and he did all of the work. He reappeared with a syringe, said something in Japanese, and drove the needle into my testicles. The pain was sharp and hard. And he disappeared again.

Fifteen to twenty minutes elapsed and he then appeared with a scalpel. Grabbing my testicle, he made an incision, cut out a piece of vas deferens, tied them off, and nonchalantly thru it over his shoulder where it stuck to the wall momentarily and then slide to the floor. Five stiches, two crisscrossed Band-aids later and he sat me upright, the whole procedure taking less than a half-hour. He handed me a piece of paper on which was written "5000 Y" which translated was about fifty dollars. I gave him the money and he said not a word and I left, never to return.

A week later I removed the stiches myself.

And the RAPCON was enticing. Every day I went to work I hoped to be assigned to Terminal, and of course it occasionally happened. The RAPCON Chief, S/M.Sgt. Burrell, was scrupulous about rotating assignments. The days, as they did when you were comfortable with yourself, flew by.

At a dining in ceremony, one evening, Alice and I sat across from a Marine Corps 1st Lt. who, after a few belts, began talking about Bobby Kennedy's epic fifty miles walk in twelve hours. He stated that no one in the room could match that, obviously referring to the Air Force part. He pissed me off but both of us in uniform prevented me from getting in his face so off I went home, got a map and found an intersection, Nudiah, just short of Kagoshima , a city to our Southeast, that was exactly twenty-five statute miles from the main gate.

Without a word to anyone, at six A.M. I left the main gate. Enroute to Nudiah, Kagoshima and return, fifty miles round trip. I ran awhile and walked, ran and walked, jogged, walked and walked.

Meanwhile, Alice, somewhat concerned, had called Bob Burrell and told him what I was doing. Bob broadcast it high and wide and they all decided to have a party that night in honor, for at least an attempt, to equal Bobby Kennedy's performance.

I reached the Nudiah intersection at 11:40, grinned, Put my name and time/date under a rock, did an about face and started back at a run. Even being in good shape, I was getting tired. I had memorized several checkpoints and timed them on my way out so coming back I could judge my progress, or lack of it. At the first checkpoint coming back I was four minutes late. I began to run. And run. And jog. At the second checkpoint half way back, I was three minutes ahead. I was elated but could feel the cramping in my legs starting. I ran.

And walked fast, and ran, and walked and walked. At the last checkpoint about ten miles from the base, I was four minutes ahead! I got pumped and began to run. The sun was starting to set on my left and that further drove me, because I knew I had to be at the gate before it set. And at this point several of my buddies passed by in a car checking on me waving and hooting.

This spurred me on. I ran, and walked and jogged and walked. Finally I was on Tudoie Street, the main drag in K-Bar which led to the main gate. I could see the gate, and several cars parked nearby. A group of friends were standing at the gate, cheering me on. I ran, hobbling, crossed the gate and collapsed in their arms. I received a hand salute from the two Air Policemen at the gate. It was 5:50 P.M.

Into the back of a car I went, off to the party and when I got there my legs had cramped so bad I could not move them and the pain was setting in. They carried me into the house and they were all there, including mama-san. Alice thru her arms around me, and Bob and the others gave pats on the head. I had two drinks and had to be supported while I attempted to walk off the cramps. I was not able to do so they eventually carried me home and put me in bed.

I never saw the Marine again .The base paper printed the exploit and I hoped the 'Jar Head' read it.

One day, as I was driving to work, I saw that the clouds were moving in and the visibility was lowering. I checked the assignment sheet and saw I was working enroute, from eight to ten termina from ten to twelve, lunch twelve to one, departure coordinator one to three and finishing with some time as final controller. The weather forecast for the day showed thunderstorms moving in about nine A.M. with visibility reduced to six miles. An easy day!

At ten A.M. I took the terminal position. At nine we had launched six F-100s on a training exercise and they were due back at about 10:40. There were eight aircraft in the terminal area and about six or seven due in within the next twenty minutes, several more due in within the half hour. And on top of these six departures were scheduled within the next half hour. I would have my hands full, and relish every minute of it. I no more than sat down when the weather took an abrupt turn, fifteen knot wind with gusts to thirty, overcast conditions at twelve hundred feet and the visibility was down to four miles It was forecasted to worsen in the next three hours. Our minimums, which is the worst weather that would still allow operations, was a three hundred foot ceiling and/or one mile visibility. At that point all traffic would have to divert to Ashiya about thirty miles northeast. Ashiya, was the only alternate with precision radar.

We were landing to the south on Runway eighteen and the weather seemed to be holding. Things went fairly smoothly for the first half hour. We were recovering at the rate of about one every six minutes and shooting the departures out on schedule.

Then things turned to shit.

The tower advised that a C-54 starting takeoff roll had blown a tire and they had no estimate when he would clear. There was a C-45 five miles on final and a F-86 about twelve miles out ready to turn in. Precision pulled the C-45 our and I controlled the F-86. I told my coordinator to have enroute alert all of their aircraft of a delay which I had already done to mine. The F86 asked for a landing estimate and not far behind was the Flight Leader of the F-100s, who also reported at fifty six miles out, twenty eight thousand feet. I could sense some problems developing and asked my coordinator to insure Ashiya was up and running, in their seats and primed, get a current weather report from them, that there was no problem with the TACAN and the radio beacon was fully functional.

About this time Bob Burrell showed up at my shoulder and asked what I needed. I told him "get me an exact time the runway would be clear." He rogered that and disappeared. I then told my coordinator to make sure enroute did not allow any "unannounced arrivals" into our airspace.

I then advised the F-86 that he would be number one for landing and requested his fuel state, he replying "thirty minute to minimum fuel," and had him hold on a TACAN fix I designed, strictly illegal, fifteen miles northeast, halfway between Ashiya and Itazuke. At twenty thousand feet. Minimum fuel simply translated as 'get on the ground now!' I sent the conventionals to our low altitude holding pattern holding pattern south of the base. I did some quick mental calculations based on what I knew of the F-100s airspeed profile. Four minutes to fly final approach. Thirteen minutes in the pattern descending from twenty thousand meant that I had to have the last F-100 on final twenty four minutes after the runway cleared.

And work I did, I glanced behind me and saw not only Bob Burrell but also the facilities officer and the F-100 squadron commander clustered with headsets on. The F-100 boss and the facility officer both had worried looks. Bob was nodding with his eyes shut. I was being monitored. Plans that I had laid in bed wrestling with trying to go to sleep in days long gone came rushing back.

I sent the 100s to the same temporary fix, holding at twenty one to twenty thousand feet describing a left handed holding pattern which would allow me to bring them in on a high descending base leg, the shortest route. To either me or Ashiya. I debated sending one to Ashiya and one to us but reserved that for a fallback position. Bob tapped me on the shoulder and said the C-54 would be clear in five minutes. I told him I wanted a second final controller with a third standing by. Startled, he said "we have never had three final controllers working at once!" I replied that today may be the time to burn the books. He again said roger and set it up.

I broadcast the runway status to all and immediately and started the F-86 in on a long descent, waited four minutes and started the first F-100 down, advising all of the jets to reach approach speed fifteen miles out. They all rogered and seemed to have caught on. Down started the third and fourth. I vectored them on a perfect, if I might say, five mile base and turned them to final at ten miles. Number four was three miles behind number three and we used the second final controller. Number five was four miles behind at ten miles, and the third final controller went to work. The last F-100 who landed, as he was parking, called and jokingly said he was declaring minimum fuel and gave me a pat on the head.

I then worked the conventionals in at five miles apart and along with six departures that had been delayed, cleared my desk. I looked up for the first time and it was noon.

Bob patted me on the arm and my relief slid in. I stood shaking and turned, seeing the F-100 and my squadron commander smiling from ear to ear. Bob took me outside and my hands were shaking so bad he had to lite me up. Many pats on the head followed.

For this I received a full course dinner for me, my family and mama-san at the Officers Club, with several F-100 jocks in attendance, I was the PACAF Airman of the Quarter and two months later I was promoted to T.Sgt. with minimum time in grade.

A reputation as the best Terminal Controller in PACAF, Pacific Air Force. It was the high point of my air traffic control career!

The Japanese Method

Our small family, with our adopted grandmother, were happy and content. Steve was six and away at kindergarten, Mike ten, at school. Alice had made a few more friends and was socializing for the first time with her best friend, Cathy, so Alice had a partner. They spent a lot of time on base shopping or the local Ginza, with occasional forays to downtown Fukuoka to sight-see.

Money was no longer a problem because of my increased military pay and the relative in expense of living in Japan. In fact, we started to save one-hundred dollars a month and eventually put enough together to get a 1954 Chevy sedan.

My days fell into a rhythm, I constructed a two by four board buried in concrete in my backyard for karate practice. Get up, work out on my Tamishawara (board striking), shower, go to work, go to karate class in Fukuoka and spend time with the family.

The second year in my karate studies, after workout, three of us went to a local tea house right around the corner. I had been there several times, and in fact I was hitting on one girl in particular. My Japanese was getting better but I was still learning a very complex language.

The two black belts and I, the brown, sitting between them, were sitting on the stools when four young Japanese men came in and sat in a booth behind us.

I heard one of them make a snide comment about the "gugakugiin" and I ignored it.

Fukuoka, like many Japanese cities, seemed to have its own political culture. Throughout Japan, after the Second World War, great importance was attached to the community, often at odds with the federal government. Many of the cities had openly adopted a political stance in opposition to their rulers. Fukuoka was one of these. Fukuoka University, where many of my fellow Karatak's studied at, was totally communist and they were very proud of their anti-western hate especially for the USA, their sentiment running deep and wide.

When I had first started studying Karate, I felt a lot of distance and contempt from some of my fellow students and thought at the time it was because I was a foreigner. It was not until my Japanese got to a point where I could converse a little, did I understand that political posture was the reason for the aloofness. In addition, after a while, they understood that I would not give up and in fact, was a "bad muther——," which they respected.

As the young girl was serving, the tea, I, in broken Japanese, made a comment about her hair which came out wrong and I found out later, was perceived as an insult to the young lady and all Japanese as well. Suddenly, my friend on my right slammed his arm out hitting me across the chest and knocked my off my stool. As I was going down the thought flashed "What the hell is this for?"

When I looked up I could see my partners in a fight with the other 4. 0ne stepped on my right hand, fracturing a bone. I sprang up and struck one of them on the side of the neck with "shuto," a blow with the edge of the hand on the carotid artery and in amazement, saw his eyes become unfocused as he slid to the floor. My God, I thought, this shit really works! It was over in short order.

I found out that my partner, out of the corner of this eye, saw them get up and come over, obviously with ill intent. He knocked me off to give himself room to move and to protect me. Two of the assailants were still down, both groggy, the others had fled. We apologized to the owner, who had come up front, who said he had called the police. And very shortly, four Junsan (police) walked through the door, very carefully. After talking to us, the owner and the girl, they decided to let us go, but warned us about keeping our karate in the dojo. The two bums that remained were hauled off in cuffs.

About the same time, I was promoted to T.Sgt.

I found out much later that the F-100 Group Commander and the Itazuke Base Commander both wrote a recommendations to the PACAF Promotion Board on my behalf.

Very shortly thereafter we received an invitation to move to Brady Airfield, the location of actual on-base housing. We all hopped in the car and went out to take a look. The housing area, BX, theater and commissary were all in one mile square area, one side on the bluffs overlooking the Tsuchima Straits. Again, the housing was a block, this time very long, with eight units in each, all four bedrooms and a large bath upstairs, a bath and the normal layout downstairs. The room size was almost double what we had lived in. The yard was enormous. Brady was about fifteen miles from Itazuke so the driving time was about equal. The only problem was mama-san, who had been with us for a year. We finally found a bus service, which I paid for, so she could work with us three days a week. That solved, I dug up my tamishiwara post and we moved in.

We had no more than settled when I got a phone call from the Squadron Exec PACAF had been requested by MAAGV (Military Assistance Group, Vietnam) to provide some instructional personnel to the Vietnamese government. One part was for terminal approach controllers. He advised it would be a sixty day TDY, under austere conditions at full per diem, the Vietnamese government providing meals and quarters. I ask him to repeat the part about full per diem, at that time twelve dollars per day, and he did so. He also advised that the per diem could be paid in advance. I could not pass up the extra seven hundred.

So with Alice grumbling, but seven hundred richer, in Febuary 1963, I frantically gathered up all of the training material and technical specifications we had, said goodbye to my family, and hopped on a C-54 bound for Vietnam.

A little background is probably in order. Tan Son Nhut was originally constructed in the 1920s by the French and was severely remodeled later in 1995. They had parallel runways, 07-25, I believe, both about ten thousand feet. And of course the war was raging at this point and the political structure was very shaky. There were tons of various commands, including TACP's (tactical air control parties) which, to some degree had priority on departure because these mission were direct fire support.

It became, in 1965, the busiest airport in the world.

The CPN-18 modified Search Radar had been installed late in 1962, and was maned by USAF and some Vietnamese AF controllers. The same with precision radar, but they needed out of facility instructors to accelerate the learning curve of the Viet controllers. We were quartered and taught in some low French buildings on, I believe the eastern side of the base, just off the approach end of runway twenty-five. And by the way, for the uninitiated, all runways are named for the magnetic heading they align with.

The quarters were two to a room and the cuisine was basically French/Vietnamese. The classrooms were surprising well appointed, each having a blackboard, and believe it or not, chalk. There were two amphitheaters for our use, and of course, a twenty-four hour mess hall. The area was fenced and patrolled, and we were instructed not to leave the compound. I was assigned a classroom with twelve Vietnamese AF Lt. students, beginning two days after our arrival and seven days a week. The Lts. had been thru the basic ATC Course, some at Keesler, but most in-country.

My first question was the language and I was told that the students spoke "sufficient" English to control traffic. Down the hall was a mockup RAPCON well laid out but unresponsive. Luckily I had brought several boxes of AF Form 1361s and 62s arrival and departure strips. I frantically, in long hand, all night long, built a lesson plan that outlined various subjects and the order I would teach them. And gave them to the secretary they had provided. I also requested they provide the strip racks. And so it began.

Classes were ten hours a day, seven days a week, with a two hour break for lunch. The first day, I handed out the lesson plans, explained the strips and the significance of the boxes and what was entered in them. I also explained that they were expected to study at night, and come to class the next day prepared to review the previous instruction. Next on the list came separation, conventional and radar, holding patterns, hand off procedure, coordination with other positions and entities and all of the other components necessary for a terminal controller to function. At the end of the course, we went down to the mockup and played controller/pilot. In fact we did a lot of that. I started having a coordinator, controller and one student play aircraft, gradually building up to a point that the controller could work eight inbound aircraft and two departures.

Anyway, it took about three weeks to get the first class cooked and served. I had one Lt. that, although I spent several evenings with him, he could not grasp the concept so I worked far into the early morning hours. He finally got it. I had a second class starting the same day the first class had graduated. And a third; MAAGV advised me this would be my last class, they now had enough terminal people, and when I was finished, I could go home. I pounced on this.

It was the only time I had been separated from Alice and had been faithful. Alice and I were beginning to have serious problems. She resented my time spent at the dojo, and continually harped on the money situation, always wanting more. And she started accusing me of having affairs which she always suspected but never proved, even accusing me of having a dalliance with Joyce, her part time sister.

But, as in all marriages, things cooled after a while. Thank God Alice found some additional friends to pal around with, along with Cindy. This seemed to keep her satisfied, busy and occupied. Our sex life went from practically nonexistent to on a rare occasion.

One day, with the boys pestering me, the three of us set of to explore the beach under the ninety-foot bluffs. He kicked around on the beach, saw some crab and a whale far out to sea. We were having a lot of fun chasing each other in the warm sand, when the boys asked if they could climb the bluff. I said, "Hell let's do it," and we started. Mike scuttled up in a hurry, Steve took his time, with me on the rocks below hollering encouragements. When Steve got almost to the top he ran out of any hand holds. He was frozen in place and beginning to cry. Mike peered over the top trying to comfort him. He reached down to Steve but came up short. So up the bluffs went Pop. I got next to Steve, and looking up about three feet above and on top of the bluff, was an old rusted drainage pipe, about six inches across, extending out about two feet. I told Steve, on the count of three, he was to grab me around the shoulders use me as a foothold and scramble up me to the top. I counted "one two three!" Steve reached out, grabbed hold of me and stepping on my shoulders and with Mikes help, got to the top. With them peering over the top down on me, I mentally crossed my fingers, jumped up and got hold of the pipe which held! I struggled up and the three of us sat down laughing, and watched the sun set. One of the best time I have ever had with the boys.

And as it happens, my life again changed gears when, in March of 1964, after originally volunteering in 1958, I received orders to curtail my overseas assignment and, in June proceed to McChord AFB, Washington for assignment to a Combat Control Team.

A Parallel Universe

In June of 1964, I arrived at McChord and we went into guest quarters. Being on leave, I did not have to check in immediately so the first order of business was to buy a car. What I thought would be a real headache turned out to be a simple matter and the second day I bought a Ford four door sedan, on time payments.

Next a place to live. Again, I got lucky because the car salesman had bought his home in Lakewood, a McChord suburb, and he put me in contact with the agent.

Two days later, I bundled the family in our car and headed for the address, 6403 Lakewood Drive, to meet him and look at a couple houses. We viewed a few and decided on the first one, a flat-roofed, wood construction four bedroom home very similar to our first one in Scott. The school that both boys would attend was two blocks away. The rooms were a little small, but not bad. It had a big fenced in back yard, and unknown in those days, came with a year's guarantee on the water heater, air and heating unit. I dusted off my GI bill and it was ours. We arranged to have our belongings delivered the next week and once they arrived, we set up shop.

And in the meantime I had checked in and had met most of the McChord team: Capt. Pitzer, M.Sgt. Bill Strickland, Bill Winters, Fish Herron, Les Hall, John Sadon, and a couple others. Sgt. Strickland told me to take all the time I needed to get my family squared away and then I would begin my training, with three weeks at jump school. He asked me if I was fit, and did I have any experience. I told him I felt I was fit, and mentioned a little of my parachuting experiences, saying only that I had made a couple freefalls several years ago. Right from the start I sensed some animosity, and so, as to not attract attention, I said little of my previous experiences.

The kids started school immediately and the first two days were hectic making that adjustment. And Alice and I found a used furniture store and bought the bedroom stuff, a dining table with no chairs, a couch, and that was it, fully furnished and comfortable. However, there was a price.

The first six months I was at McChord were hectic and stressful to say the least. A major problem had developed because of the number of schools I needed to attend to become qualified. As I recall, I believe there were nine, ranging in time from two to seven weeks. In fact, in the 90s the Air Force, who only required a four year enlistment, upped it to six for combat control because of the training required. Alice was constantly complaining about Mike and Steve's conduct, and the time I spent away from home and insisted it was not fair to her. My response was that it was just temporary, as soon as I finished my schooling I would be home more often...perhaps. Our marriage was going downhill.

One day, with our MRC broken down, John Sadon and I were working a heavy equipment drop with a three quarter ton from the motor pool. It was my habit of visual determining a release point and seeing how close the aircraft actual came to it. This day, having parked the three quarter ton on the IP, about half way through, an aircraft launched an A-22 at the spot I had visualized. As the load was about 300 feet, John turned to me and said, "Should we move it?" to which I replied, "—— it!"

The A-22 smashed the cab of the truck. We had to call the aircraft and relay the message to the motor pool.

And I guess now, with tales of daring do, is a good time to bring up RECONDO School.

After I had been at McChord for a short time, I realized that my ideas pertaining to tactical capabilities and challenges were not appreciated. They were, in fact scoffed at. I was the 'new kid on the block' and my questions about field operations amounted to nothing. The normal response was "we ain't in the Army." For all of the schools we attended, there was not one which dealt with field operations. This was not what I expected or wanted.

I went to Capt. Pitzer and asked for a quota to Rangers School. He checked back later and said none was available but he could get me into RECONDO School. He explained what it was and that it was perhaps even more difficult than Rangers School. To go to RECONDO School you needed to have been an airborne squad leader in the Army, for one year, and highly recommended by your platoon leader. I told him I could hack it and he agreed to try and get me a slot. I went to the base library and got everything I could find on platoon operations and expanded my horizons greatly, doing the studying quietly and away from the team.

I realized also, along with my complete lack of knowledge, that being the first AF grunt ever to go to RECONDO School would carry some heavy penalties...it did. A month or so later, the Capt. told me that I was scheduled for RECONDO School next week.

And so I reported in for RECONDO School at Ft. Campbell, KY. The Army ranger Sgt. checking me in, looked at me and slyly said, "Air

Force, huh, ain't ever had any a you for breakfast. You ain't gonna make it, save us all a problem and just go home." I told him I planned on finishing his (expletive) course.

The physical and academic phases were hard, the academic most of all, because I had no actual squad experience. We began, I believe, with about forty students and twenty-eight finished the course. On the first day, a couple rangers called me out and had me drop and give them fifty pushups. I did so and they got in my face swearing, "YOU GONNA QUIT, WE WILL MAKE THAT HAPPEN, YOU PIECE OF SHIT." This was often repeated during the course. The procedure was that when you talked to an instructor, you had to start with "Ranger, etc etc." They ordered me to drop and give another fifty. I could only do thirty. They again got in my face and screamed, "AIRDALE, WE GOT YOUR BALLS IN OUR FIST, YOU AIN'T GONNA MAKE IT!" I screamed, "RANGER, GO(EXPLETIVE) YOURSELF!"

There was stunned silence. They then ordered me to rejoin the class. I realized that if there was going to be any "special training," I would catch it. The first week I was given the M-60 to carry on the five mile run, in addition to my M-16, and ordered to strip the M-60 that night. Hell, I had no idea how it worked must less how it was field stripped. So after the night classes, which ended at nine thirty, a couple of my fellow students came to my aid, and a little after two A.M. we had it all cleaned and re-assembled. And at four A.M. we were up and at it again, six days a week.

And it continued on. We were swinging across a stream on a ropes and the Rangers were telling the class when to release so that you landed dry on the opposite bank. When it came my turn, the command was issued as I was over the middle. I let go of the rope and got wet. One of the staff, at least twice a day would 'talk' to me about 'go'n home.' During the rappelling phase I was always first off the mockup and screamed at for being too slow on descent. The helicopter rappel was a repeat of the mockup. And on it went.

During the last several days of the seven week course, came the resistance to interrogation phase. We made an assault on a camp and three of us "were captured." I was strung up on a crossbar and beaten in the stomach by a ranger named Gomez. He insisted I talk and every time I refused, he hit me in the stomach. When the blood circulation in my hands began to cease, they would bring me down and tie me to a post and the interrogation would continue. When my circulation returned to normal, back on the crossbar I would go, "RANGER, GO (EXPLETIVE) YOURSELF."

Another student who had expressed a fear of snakes was strapped to his cot, and a small tree Boa laid on his chest with the threat of stuffing it up his ass. He moaned and screamed but did not talk. I don't know what happened to the third guy.

Eventually came graduation day, Ranger Gomez came up and extended his hand, we shook, he said, "good job Airdale." I responded, "(expletive) you Gomez." I would see him occasionally as he worked as a bouncer at the Airbase Enlisted Club and I always bought him a beer. Jose, would respond with a big grin and raise his fist in the air.

I had been gone about two months and when I got home, I found that Alice's sister had moved in and that Alice had taken a job at the NCO Club at Ft. Lewis, down the road a bit. I was not pleased with these arrangements but could do little about it. Money was not the problem, most of my trips paid full per diem so we had the money. I think she just resented having the kids and was striving for her own identity.

Les Hall, Bill Winters, and I became tight as they were into freefalling. I of course, would relate my tales of derring-do while packing parachutes and they would respond. As often as possible we would talk the Army Aviation Group at Ft. Lewis into flying us. More often than not they would and the freefalls added up.

One day we convinced Capt. Pitzer to try it. I believe Bill was the jumpmaster, Les and I were at the impact point. The Capt. deplaned where he should have and fell, and fell and fell. I said, "Shit," and a canopy appeared as he disappeared at the tree line. When we found him, somewhat shook, he admitted he had not pulled his ripcord completely out of the pocket and went for his reserve. That was his last freefall.

And my nefarious conduct had not changed. On every trip, if there was a possibility I went for it. In Moses Lake I met a woman who worked in a flower shop, named Pat Enzler. Every time I came to 'Moses hole,' I would find her and the romance was on. The same with a waitress in Fort Knox, a bank teller at Ft. Campbell and a car wash girl in the Mojave.

I finished all of the schools, was pronounced qualified, but the missions increased, requiring more time on the road. And Alice was spending more time at the club than was necessary, so I was told, and she was spending a lot of time with a particular Sgt.—the NCO Club Manager.

While at Moses Lake, on a beautiful cloudless day, Les and I decided to do a 'buddy jump,' where you left the aircraft with each holding on to the others lift web. Bill and I had done it the week before at Ft. Lewis and it worked fine. I was so elated, during the jump I had reached over and kissed Bill on the cheek and he turned red.

We left the door and immediately went 'z,' a parachutist slang for an uncontrolled position. In the struggle I had gotten my whole left arm under his lift web. We struggled and I saw Les glance down at his altimeter and he pulled. My arm came ripping out from behind his harness and I pulled, swung once and impacted. When Les pulled, he had scrapped my watch and my wedding ring off my left arm and finger!

Fifty years later he sent me a replacement for both, which I have up on my wall.

By this time, Alice had had enough. When I came home from a TDY, my clothes and suitcases were on the bed. She and I were alone in the house, her sister having taken the kids out for a while. And she issued her edict.

Either I resign from combat control and spend all of my time at home, or she wanted a divorce. I tried to explain how important this function was for me but she would have none of it. I started to suspect I had a rival. In any event I tried to explain that I could not, even if I wanted to, just walk out. It would take time for me to be reassigned. She didn't want to hear it, so off I went to the barracks, leaving her the car, house, and $200 a month in child support. She filed for a divorce which I did not contest and it was granted. The car had been paid off, and the house payment was fifty-three dollars, a month, so with her job she should be all right. And I went out and bought a little red Alpha convertible.

A month later, in January of 1966, I received orders assigning me to the new team at Travis, an assignment stewarded by, I have always believed, Capt. Pitzer. We had many conversations after I returned from RECONDO School about the unpopularity of small unit tactic training for combat controllers. The McChord team, with perhaps one exception, were dead set against it. Their perception was that an Army security element would always be there to protect CCT in a tactical environment. It was my position that we would someday operate as an integral part of a SEAL or SF unit, and this, of course, has come to pass.

So I packed my bags, jumped into my little red Alpha, and drove to California.

In Febuary 1966, I shook hands with Capt. Arlon Jahnke, an ex-T.Sgt., and met the few that were there, Hap Saunders being one of the first, not only first but one of the brightest. We were quartered in a hangar on the flight line with the aerial port delivery sections, without much room, none for a packing table. The team was starting to build, so in a hurry I had to construct a guide to our day to day activates and training, including manning the one drop zone we had, at the time, Sloughhouse, outside Sacramento. One of the first things I did was to convince Capt. Jahnke, and the Assistant Team leader, Lt. Reid, that we needed to be always on full per diem, unless the order stated that we must utilize government quarters, because I remembered how short money was when I was a young airman. Finance agreed!

Next I needed a clerk and one came with the name, Al Bass, a most recent arrival, who had been a clerk before he came to us and he agreed. Al proved to be invaluable and without him the Team would not have existed. Next stop was the aerial delivery guy, another T.Sgt. I convinced him to give us room on the hangar floor for parachute storage and a packing table. He authorized this and next day I went to base supply and ordered everything we were authorized, including M-16s and .38 pistols. We were not authorized M-60s. And in they came, Gary Harwell, Hank Schaffer, K.B. Duncan, Art John, John Jenkins, Clyde Howard, Jim Hillard, Bill Warick, Joe Hawkins, John Koren, and all the rest. At top strength we were a big team, thirty-four total assigned.

Once operations and normal CCT training were covered, I turned my attention to field training and made contact with some folks, the reserve SF Team in Sacramento. The Amphibious Warfare School at Vallejo and the Force Reconnaissance Course at Coronado, California. All agreed to help if we would help them get training airlift as they required it.

The SF folks agreed to include us in all their field exercises and provide a rappelling site. I took six to the Navy school in Vallejo and wouldn't you know it, the last night Clyde Howard got drunk and there was a free for all in the ranks club. The SPs responded and we were never allowed back in the club.

I arranged for full scale team deployment to the USMC Recon Course in Coronado, a two week course involving tactics but primarily teaching the carrying, launching and utilization of the IBS (inflatable boat small), a 750 pound rubber boat with a crew of seven. We in fact were able to launch our boats in surf after SEAL 1 decided it was too rough. The third night a fight erupted between CCT and the Marine recruits which ended in a draw. The next morning I and the Marine Sgt. Maj. were at a brace in front of the school commandant and severely criticized for our inability to control our men. All this impressed the Marines to the extent that when we were about to leave, the school Sgt. Maj. marched up to me, saluted, and presented me with his survival knife. I returned the salute and he marched off.

Shortly thereafter I received a phone call from the SF Team in Sacramento. They had been tasked to participate in an exercise against an Army hospital battalion encamped on the Fort Ord Reservation, a place we often trained at. The scenario was that the hospital had been deployed to a foreign country and had set up 'bare bones' with the normal primary and secondary defense perimeters, no towers. They had a prior commitment so they asked me if we wanted to 'play.' I jumped at the chance and they said they would provide the OPORD.

A week later it came in and I designed the mission profile, plotting their position, asked for airdrop and sent a team to the DZ six miles south of the hospital site the day prior. They were to set the DZ up covertly for a night insertion. Twelve of us, M-16s with blanks and smoke grenades, I loaded the C-141 and at nine P.M. hit the silk, formed up and moved the six miles to the pre-established recon point. I sent two patrols out to locate any perimeter and both came back in an hour with the route we needed. I issued the PLO and then set off down the road carrying the body of a dead rattlesnake in my pocket I had killed earlier and a couple fictitious rattlesnake bites in my left forearm. One of the post's roving patrols picked me up and I identified myself as a Marine Capt. separated from his unit and needing rattler bite first aid. They of course took me to the hospital unit who admitted me without question. My part was to recon the interior looking for the CP and if possible get the word back to Hap Saunders, who was in charge. After a couple hours they became suspicious and strapped me to a cot. Fortunately they did not inject any anti-venom serum, which if they had, would have made me terribly sick.

Nevertheless, at five A.M. Hap got all of the way inside of their perimeter and made a successful assault on the CP, which he had identified, on his own.

The hospital Col. took the defeat gracefully and invited us all for breakfast, which we did, road marched back to the DZ and were picked up by two busses. We were jubilant!

We had one DZ, the one at Sloughhouse, which was worked seven days a week. It was essentially A-22 equipment drops, with some personnel drops mixed in and more operations were quickly forthcoming. We needed a steady place to live near there, so I found the Stardust Motel in southeastern Sacramento which had a pool and two connected four bedroom units, I talked to Curly and Mabel, the owners, and made arraignments for us and aerial delivery to stay there. And of course, one of the other attributes was the bar next door, the name escapes me. At any time, day or night, you could find a couple of the guys knocking them down, but only after a mission.

I established PT as a daily affair after morning formation, in ranks. I would inspect, by the book, not only to insure their appearance was always exceptional, but to build esprit de corp. They always trained together, worked together, on occasion fought together or with each other, and played together. By design. I was convinced that a team needed to be exactly that and at every opportunity reinforced that. One day, during a run, an Air Police vehicle passed us honking loudly and swerved slightly in our direction. I briefed the team. The next morning, the same thing occurred, but I commanded, "Fingers up," and the APs were presented with twenty or so 'go to hell' attitudes. We never again had any problems from them.

I designed and taught a mini RECONDO School, several times. Rather than only firing for qualifications once a year, we fired every quarter. I wanted the best trained, most motivated combat control team in existence. I insisted that all of them went through the RECONDO training and all of the other 'Army' training I could find. At the end of the first year they were better trained than any other team in existence and after about a year I had the best combat control team in the Air Force! When Hank Scaffer returned from Nam he thanked me. He said without the training I had provided, he would have never been the RECONDO Honor graduate at NaTrang as he was.

I called RECONDO School and who should answer but the now 1st Sgt. Ranger Jose Gomez. After several minutes of playing catch up, I asked if I could have five slots. He checked and said he could give me three slots the next month. I took them and told him I owed him a bottle of Scotch.

And so I asked for volunteers and all raised their hands. So I selected three, Hap Saunders, Nick Genes and one other, whose name escapes me, and off they went with a bottle of Chivas.

The wing had coordinated with the 82 airborne so that two squads of troopers would come to Travis to help our jump qualifications for the navigators. As a result, Spc. 5, Joe Rodriguez, a parachute rigger, was assigned and I got to know him and his wife, Cindy, very well. Those who had family nearby, I would assign four jumps on Monday and Tuesday and then release them so they could spend time with their families. Towards the end of his ninety day TDY, he was alerted for

Nam, so he left Cindy and their daughter with her parents in Oakland and off he went.

A month or so went by and I got a phone call from Cindy who was at the main gate. Joe, on his first patrol, got hit and they had shipped him back to the hospital at Travis. I met Cindy at the hospital and we visited her husband. He was unconscious and hooked up to a breathing machine. I later learned that he was in fact, brain dead. Cindy would visit perhaps twice a week for a while and we would join up to visit, then a couple weeks went by with no contact from her.

Then she called, and I could tell she was nervous, so I went to the NCO Club to meet her. Before she could get started I told her that she and her daughter needed to get on with their life, and forget Joe. She tearfully replied she had been seeing someone, and her conscience was bothering her. I got up from the table and told her not to come back.

A couple weeks went by and I was notified that Joe had been transferred to the hospital at the Presidio, so I went down to visit him.

The ward that he was on was special, because its only patients were those who could not fend for themselves, in a room off of the ward, laid Joe and two others, all three hooked up to a breathing machine. HAAAAAH OWW, HAAAAA OWW went the machines. And there was absolute silence. I never went back.

The wing, essentially because of our small injuries, had consistently scored low on all of the IG inspections. One day, during one of these, a young 2nd Lt. presented himself and wanted to talk about our abysmal performance. While I explained that some of the field training was a little hazardous, he admitted that he always had wanted to make a parachute jump. After a little conversation, I had Bill Warick take him out behind the shed and show him some PLFs. Two nights later I put him out of a C-141.

Several weeks later, when the IG report came back, we suddenly had an "above average" rating. A couple days later I was told to report to the wing commander. He proceeded to congratulate me on our sterling ground safety report. I thanked him, saluted and as I was leaving he said, "Oh by the way Phil, with a broad grin...don't ever do something like that again." I saluted and said, "Certainly, Sir."

And my social life did not go unattended. Not knowing any ladies there, I put on my uniform and went to church, and by the second Sunday had what I had come for, several times over. I also picked up an old scagg at the Sacramento bus station and took her to the Motel and passed her around. In the meantime, the waitress at the bar, Carol Alexander and I had a brief passionate affair. She was the girl who I drunkenly thought had three nipples, but found the next morning, the one in the center one was a mole. Some more Travis stories before I set off for Europe.

I was able to be friends and Boss with many, especially Hap and Art John. Art, who would cruise with me in the Alpha, one day at sixty miles per hour, deciding to take my top down and of course it blew off. Hap and his beautiful wife Cindy were special. And they helped me out when I most needed it, watching Steve and Mike while I was gone.

John Jenkins came to us without having completed jump school, so after a couple days, we put him out of a C-124. He said he loved it. And we eventually got him a slot at jmp school.

One day at formation, Jim Hillard showed up with a huge black eye. On close questioning, Hap volunteered that they had got in an argument and he had smacked him. They had been and would always be very close friends. Gary Harwell and Art John, were almost run over by a tow truck, followed it and beat the shit out of the driver. And on and on. They were tough and aggressive, like me, because that's what they knew I wanted.

We had, in a glass cage, a twelve foot tree Boa as a pet. His name was Sam and he had made his five qualifying jumps around the neck of his particular host. At one point the guys took him to the motel with them and early in the morning, Art John decided Sam needed some time in the pool. As they were basking away, a grandmother with her granddaughter also decided to take a dip, and then saw the boa in the water, screamed and the grandmother fainted. Eventually things were okay but Sam no longer was allowed out to play.

Several months later Lt. Reid was sent to Jungle Survival School in Panama and decided Sam needed some companionship so he brought another Boa aboard the civilian airliner bringing him home. The Boa was in a handbag at Bob's feet. Halfway home the bag moved and his seat companion asked what was in the bag. Bob reached down and uncoiled the snake, sending everyone into a panic. Needless to say, when the report got back to the wing commander, we almost lost an outstanding young officer. Regardless, Sam got a partner, Samantha.

One night sitting in the bar next to the Stardust, a couple attractive well-dressed ladies walked in and took a table. Bill Warick and I strolled over, asked them to dance, bought drinks and had a good time. The one I was interested in was named Jeannie Gruman. Closing time came and I offered to take Jeannie home. She agreed and I did so. As she got out, I made a date for Friday night to take her and her buddy to San Francisco, and I asked if they were married and she grinned and said yes. I told her that Bill and I would pick them up at six P.M.

Bill and I put our uniforms on, he lied to his wife, and we picked the girls up in his station wagon. We thought, to have fun, we would pay for the night with dollar bills, so each of us had $150 in ones. Halfway to San Francisco, we pulled in for a drink and of course paid with the $1 bills. And we did Fisherman's Wharf and several afterhours clubs up Royal! Years later, I stopped in and the bartender, same one, remembered the incident.

A couple months went by and our affair remained constant. I found out she was married to an officer who was TDY a lot and had three small children.

Anyway, I had forgotten to get someone from aerial delivery to feed our snakes. When we returned, they were restlessly curled at opposite ends of their sandy beach and I realized they were probably hungry. I got a mouse, opened the top and dropped the mouse in. Samantha made a full strike at the mouse, missed and got Sam behind the head and tore off about a half-dollar size piece of flesh. I got Sam out of the cage and had Al Bass call the base veterinarian. There was no answer. I thought, the Flight Surgeon takes care of us, hell why not? So I grabbed one of the guys and the jeep and we all hotfooted it to the hospital.

Unfortunately we parked in an area that required we go through the pregnancy waiting room, which we did at the trot, holding Sam in my arms. Screams, magazines thrown in the air and pure panic marked our passing. The flight surgeon came around the corner, and seeing Sam, he dryly asked what his aeronautical rating was. They took Sam in and placed him in isolation (a bottom draw), called the veterinarian who came down, and they worked on him until ten pm, when Sam died, apparently from blood poisoning. Two days later Sam made his last airborne exit, by himself, from a C-141 at six thousand feet over Sacramento.

One day Alice called and begged me to take Mike and Steve, who were both getting in trouble. I reminded her that she had stipulated in the divorce decree that I could not have the boys unless I was married. She begged me to find a way out.

I dug up my old note book and found Patricia Enzler's phone number and called her, asking, if, after two years, she remembered me. She said she did and the next words out of my mouth was "will you marry me and come to California for thirty days." There was stunned silence.

And then she came back on line and laughingly accepted my proposal. I told her I would pick her up in five days, take her to Cour de Lane Idaho, which had no waiting period, marry her, come to Tacoma pick up my two and bring her and her two children to Travis. And with a giggle, she agreed to my terms of endearment.

I called around and rented a house, borrowed Bill Warick's Station Wagon, called Alice and briefed her, and off I went to get my new temporary bride.

And it went off like clockwork. Patricia found a job in a florist shop in Fairfield, just outside the Base, and we cohabitated. And of course I was still seeing Jeannie on the side. At the end of the thirty-day period, I told her that was it and I would not be coming back. She naturally had a fit, screamed and cried. I reminded her what I had told her and she said she thought I was just kidding.

So I and the kids moved in with Hap and Cindy so that she could watch the kids while I was TDY and we lived there for a couple months.

In the meantime, I went to Tijuana, Mexico and got a Mexican divorce from Patricia. Two months went by with relative calm and I, of course, was still seeing Jeannie anytime her husband was TDY, and Jeannie was becoming more dissatisfied with her husband. And then the Air force decided to screw with me and I received orders for RAF Lakenheath, England, 1st Aerial Port CCT. I had forty-five days to report. Now what!

I had two boys that I could not and would not give up, and no wife to care for them while I did Europe. One night I mentioned my quandary to Jeannie and she proposed a solution. She would divorce her husband and marry me and off to England we would go. And another adventure began. Patricia threatened to blow the whole deal, so Jeannie offered Patricia her Volkswagen if she would not cause problems, and Patricia agreed. So I was brought from bondage for a 1962 Beetle.

And SMS Joe Willard came in to relieve me. Joe turned out to be the best NCOIC I ever had. He had the 'command posture' and he was admired and respected by all.

By this time the team had earned a reputation throughout the base as 'bad muther——s,' a reputation not missed by the squadron 1st Sgt. One day he called Joe and explained that he was having serious trouble with the people in the barracks. They were sleeping in, the place was a constant mess and there was no cohesion amongst them. Other Section NCOICs had approached the problem but had no result. Joe told the 1st Sgt. "he would take a look at the problem."

Joe summoned K.B.Duncan and myself and explained the situation, and that we would visit the barracks tomorrow at 0830 and 'eliminate' the problem.

And so we did. The barracks were still the old, double bunk, two footlocker, two wall locker segments. At 0830 we stormed in, with our best drill instructor voices and manners, tipped over bunks, emptied wall and foot locked, locked two airmen in the latrine, and physically 'corrected' two of them, K.B. slapping one in the face repeatedly. When we left there was dead silence, with the occupants hard at work repairing the 'discussion.' The 1st Sgt. advised several weeks later that he now had the model barracks and decorum.

And off to Lackenheath I went.

The Flirtation

Enroute to Lakenheath from Dover, I sat next to an attractive forty year old who introduced herself as, I believe, Lillian Byrd, who was coming back from visiting her sister and was rejoining her husband. We had a very deep, wide ranging and steady conversation. As we were deplaning at Mildenhall, I asked for her phone number. Smilingly she declined and kissing me on the cheek walked away. I never saw her again.

At Lackenheath were D.R. Smith, Arlon Jahnke, Lennie Cade, Oscar Dillingham, Lou Boone, Leo Whitikar, Jerry Rice and a couple more. All good folks. We were there only about a month, when we re-located to a large hangar at RAF Mildenhall. And I bought D.R. Smiths car, since he was going home.

Almost immediately I was able to get off base housing, a four bedroom unit in the village of Mildenhall. It was a very nice two story home, freshly painted. The furniture provided by the base was first class and so I immediately sent for my family.

Jeannie and the kids were very pleased. The school for all of them was about five blocks away, and of course it was English and the kids were a rarity and very popular. She immediately met several neighbors and of course, the team wives, and was in her element. Bridge on Tuesdays became the norm, and unlike her predecessor, she did not mind the TDY.

Several weeks after arriving, when Capt. Jahnke, who had preceded me from Travis, was TDY, I attended the first wing ops meeting. It was a monthly affair that aerial port was required to attend. I walked in and sat down at the end of the room full of officers. At the end of the table was a short grizzled full colonel, who motioned me up. From his desk plate I could see he was director of operations. I snapped to, he rose and put out his hand. His name tag said BYRD and I said to myself, oh shit, thinking of course of Lillian.

At the end of the meeting, he asked me to stay behind. We had a get together where he asked me to tell him about myself. In the course of the conversation he asked if I had sat next to his wife when I rotated in. I gulped and said yes. He said she had sang my praises. That's all he ever said. We bonded almost immediately and from that point on, if there was an airdrop/LZ/EZ or almost any other Op that the wing was involved in, I was involved too, I believe he had a unofficial agreement with Capt. Janhke where he could 'borrow' me. Because of him I had several adventures that a T.Sgt. normally doesn't get into. These are what makes this period in my life one of the best ever.

A month after meeting Col. Byrd, Capt. Janke told me to go to Wing OPS and brief a Col. from Germany. I took our radio maintenance man, Gary Downing with me, in case there were detailed questions about com. We walked in and was introduced to Col. John Singlaub, and two Majors. Col. Singlaub was short, with very short hair, a chest of medals and a Ranger tab on his arm. He was the Seventh Army Airborne Brigade Commander in Germany.

We snapped too, and I introduced us. We then proceeded with the briefing, on CCT including drop/landing and extraction measurements and markings, IP and terrain minimums, history, capabilities, etc. and threw in a little RECONDO phraseology: order of battle, FEBA, PWO etc. I sat down and Gary did about ten minutes on com. I stood, asked if he had any questions, he asked a couple about timing points, I answered, saluted and we left.

A couple hours later the wing called the squadron CO and we got a pat on the head. In passing, this is the same Singlaub that a couple years later was Maj. Gen. Singlaub, Korean Commander, who refused to reduce his troop strength and then criticized President Jimmy Carter and was forced out. He then got involved with the Iran-Contra affair, Ollie North, and a few other things. I was destined to meet him again.

In October I was ordered to Eighth Infantry Rose Barracks, Bad Kruznach, Germany as J-3 air staff, in support of pathfinder express, a joint airborne/Spanish Army exercise commanded by Col. Singlaub. My boss was a C-123 driver, Capt. Joe Sorenson. We went over the OPSORD sentence by sentence, paying particular attention to the Air-drop Order of Battle. Although the DZ was well defined, on the southeast coast of Spain, Albacete, we did not have any photographs. I contacted J-2 and they said they would check on it.

Six days prior to the Drop, I got a phone call from Col. Byrd. He stated that someone had changed the route, now requiring that they fly over France, which was prohibited airspace since de Gaulle had kicked everyone out. Joe was out of the office so I ran upstairs and reported to Col. Singlaub what Col. Byrd had said. He started a slow burn, saying it had not happened.

At this point his chief of staff, Col. Kelly, walked in and admitted making the request for change. I was dismissed and as I left I heard Col. Singlaub's voice raise about four octaves, as did everyone in the building. I briefed Joe and called Col. Byrd back. By this time I had learned a lot about JTF and their complexity...and their personalities. And, J-2 could not find any photos of the DZ. I started checking with NATO and could not find where the DZ had never been surveyed. I immediately sensed a problem and told Joe. He agreed, but there was little at this late date that we could do about it.

Three days prior to drop, about six of us were sent to Albecete as the advanced party to make sure everything was right and establish a com center. I hopped in the Jeep and drove out to the DZ with a Spanish Army Major. Lo and behold, there was a telephone pole about 200 yards up from the IP with wires diagonally across the DZ I called Joe who was told by the Col. to "get rid of it." I then asked the Major if he had access to any demolitions and he said he thought he did. I asked him to provide sixty feet of D Cord (PETN), or one-quarter block C-3 or 4, the M-3 cap and the igniter (thanks to RECONDO School) which he did. Returning that evening I put four wraps of the cord around the post, six inches down, set up the system and blew it. Putting the local phone subscribers out of business temporarily. We towed it and the wires off the DZ, I marked the hole with a red VS 17, and reported back to Joe what I had done.

The day before the drop, the Col. arrived and he, I, and two others flew the route from the IP over the DZ. He was satisfied and grinned at me. The drop came off, with Bill Winters and the Wiesbaden team controlling, and I returned to Mildenhall via a small single engine aircraft sent from England just for me, courtesy of Col. Byrd.

I arranged to take the team to Abington, the home of the British Jump School which, for us, strangely, was run by the RAF, who also provided all jumpmasters. The British, because of the notoriously bad weather, conducted all of their jump school inside a large hangar. There was the tethered balloon from which we would all make our five qualifying jumps. Because of England's notorious bad weather, they used the balloon for their jump requirements. Three RAF sergeants would take this balloon throughout England to provide a jump platform for the reserve airborne units. I had a chance to talk to all three and they absolutely loved their assignment, because it paid full per diem all of the time!

The RAF briefed us. They would inflate the balloon and it would rise to forty feet, at which time five of us, including the RAF jump-master, would board the gondola. It was an oblong weaved basket affair, rising only to waist level. The flight up, if I can use that term loosely, was very pleasant, the gondola gently swinging in the English early morning air. At one end was a door which would be opened when we reached 800 feet. The jumpmaster would perform a final equipment check and out we would go, on his command.

I, being the ranking Sgt. went first. I hooked up, the Jumpmaster opened the door and he tapped me out. There is nothing quite like falling straight down and hearing the parachute system deploy. We each made our five, the last two from the trapdoor, and were presented with our RAF jump wings and adjourned to the Sgt.'s Mess (their club) for fun and frolic.

At home, thing were going well. I had cautioned my boys not to cause Jeannie any problems and they seemed to be heeding my advice. Mike and Steve on one of their exploratory trips, found an abandoned house with a beautiful eighteenth-century mantle clock which they brought home. It today sits on my living room. They were snuggled up in a warm home, enjoyed their environment and were getting to know each other. In 1968, Mike was sixteen, Cathy was thirteen, Steve eleven, Susy nine, and Jimmy seven. All were making good grades and had acclimatized beautifully.

And I never heard from Alice or the boys, David and Donald. Per-haps because the child support checks had never wavered.

On weekends, we would all jump in the station wagon and visit var-ious historic landmarks, Stonehenge being one of the first. Several times, Jeannie and I got a sitter and we would go off somewhere, once to London, where we spent the weekend. As guests of The Artists Rifles, 21 SAS.

I decided it was time for Jeannie and I to get loose for a couple days so I took a twenty day leave and flew to Wiesbaden Air Base, stayed with Bill Winters and his wife for a couple days, road the train to Paris, stayed for two days, via train to Marseilles, thence tour bus to Monaco, where I lost $200 and Jeannie lost $300 .We got back on the train to Wein, Switzerland, boarded the Rhine river cruise boat up through Basil and Mannheim to Cologne. We spent the day there sightseeing and then boarded the train to Calais. At Calais we made reservations to ride the two-hundred-foot long Channel Crossing Ferry. And a sign said it would be clear sailing.

At eight A.M. we boarded the Ferry for the twenty-six mile trip to Dover, which was scheduled to take three and a half hours and it was crowded, apparently always so. We had gone no more than five miles when the sky opened and the winds started. The boat rocked not only side to side but by the bow, the waves becoming higher by the minute. Jeannie said she didn't feel well so I attempted to get her to the center of the ship, where gyrations would be minimal, but it was blocked with sick standing people, throwing up over the board. By this time waves, as subsequently reported, were fourteen feet. There was the beginning of panic in the air. Men and women were both crying out loud in fear.

Everyone was sick, and it was so crowded that most could not get to the rails. People began shoving each other and stepping on the children. None of the crew were anywhere to be seen. It was a scene right out of "The Inferno."

I finally shouldered my way to the rail, grabbed one life vest got Jeannie into it and put her in front of me with my arms around her grasping the rail, so she was somewhat protected.

Seven hours later we docked at Dover. It was later reported as the largest storm of the season. I grabbed our baggage and snuck on the next train to London. We stayed there for two days, partying with the 21 SAS and thence returned to Mildenhall.

We also, along with the drop zones in England, would work a number of DZ/LZ in Germany. Generally I would assign three guys to an operation, and everything went along fine. In fact, the only serious problem I had was as a result of working a German DZ, at Kaiserslautern.

After the drop was over, three of us, Oscar Dillingham, another who I do not remember, and myself stopped off in the Army NCO Club for a beer. The three of us came in and took a table next to one already occupied by five or six tankers. As we walked in I could tell that we attracted attention, first because we were Air Force and secondly because we had berets.

It was not long before one of the tankers, announced that "Guys with funny hats shouldn't be allowed in the Club." I looked up and stared at him. He said, in a loud voice, "What the (expletive) are you looking at, you wit da queer stuff on your head." I smiled at him and stood up, walked over to him with my hand out as if to shake his, he started to stand and I introduced him to Mr. Shuto, this time to the eyes and when he reached up to them, kicked him in the balls. As he went down I grabbed his shirt and dragged him out the nearby fire door. Outside I put the boot to him, walked back inside to where the other tankers sat, and smiled at them. They all ignored me and I sat down for another beer. As we were finishing it, the Army MPs came in, and after much pointing and talking, I was issued a citation for disorderly conduct and ordered out of the club, never to return.

There was something wrong between Jeannie and I. As hard as I tried, even with my great deal of sexual experience, she became less sexually responsive. She became harsher with my children, and easier with hers. She would go for long periods without conversation, and stare blankly out of the window, or at an inanimate object. And the trips to London, Oxford, and Dublin did not seem to make a difference. And then she would snap back, smiling and gushy as she was, and become sexually aggressive. I convinced myself it was only my guilty conscience. You play, you pay.

I was then sent to NATO at Casteau, Belgium and served on a committee trying to codify AirOPS definitions between NATO and the US, normally a captain's slot. I believe the document was STANAG 3570 .The European military did not have a CCT. A designated Army airborne unit would be tasked to provide that function. One of the side events was that after the Soviet invasion of Czechoslovakia a couple years prior, it was found that no tentative *DZ/LZ's* had been determined. I asked the chairman, a German major, to send a request to HQ USAF in essence directing our CCTs to have the surveying duty. We never got a response.

However, this assignment allowed me to meet a Norwegian special operations major who invited me to attend the "winter course," north of Oslo. So I grabbed a couple of the guys, I think Gary and Leo and off we went to a three week course, where we all got a chance to put on climbing gear and ski cross country. The climb was average in difficulty, a six thousand foot mountain, one short portion a glacier, which required the use of crampons and pitons.

As usual, I was looking around for a unit we could train with, and fell upon the British SAS located at Hereford, England. They are generally conceded to be the premier special operations unit in the world, the granddaddy of us all, **and** are a fascinating unit.

I went to Hereford to see what was possible. 21SAS Regiment was the only regular unit and was at Hereford. 22 SAS and 23 SAS were reserves, located at Sloan Square in London and Dundee, Scotland respectively. Each regiment was composed of four squadrons, A, B, C, and F specializing in one type of strategic operations, and then cross trained. D and E Squadrons "did not exist." I sat in the NCO Club with Sgt. Maj. Larry Smith and another Sgt. who briefed me. Later I read of the exploits of Larry Smith. He had an outstanding career and had established his bona fides in Malaysia and Borneo in the 1950s. Stone cold killers.

Their selection course, which they ran twice a year was a killer, and I mean that literally. Only ten out of sixty would pass, and they suffered one fatality a class, usually because of dehydration. To make this more amazing, the enlisted recruits had to have served at least one tour in the British 1st Abn. Corp. so they were already tough and skilled fighters. The commissioned did not have that requirement and it showed. Only one out of nine commissioned volunteers made the course.

So we went to the training area in Hereford and I got my first exposure in fast rope, a rappelling technique that did not require a Swiss seat. You merely slid down a one inch thick rope as fast as you could manage. For some reason, the Brits did not like the idea of trapping the rope between your feet to help control the speed of descent. Sgt. Maj. Smith told me they could insert a ten man team in eight seconds. Wow!

Each recruit was given a canteen and expected to resupply themselves enroute. A few did not. This resulted in the fatality, which the SAS accepted as reasonable losses. Their selection course was in the Brecons, Wales, and the 'hill' was called Pene-fan. Traversing this hill, a thirty degree climb, 2,500 feet on shale, four times in twenty-four hours with a sixty pound pack was the standard. And I went to their three day HALO 'orientation,' made two jumps, one from nine thousand, a practice HALO, and one HALO from seventeen thousand. I could go on forever, but if you're interested, Google them.

Anyway, they agreed to help us. In turn, with Col. Byrds authorization, I gave them his phone number and he promised to provide some of their training airlift. And of course I found a girlfriend there in Hereford, who would accompany me to the Sgt.'s Mess, which was their club, every Saturday night, which absolutely rocked until the wee hours of the morning. I do not know what it was, but the British ladies were the best I ever had. I had a ball! I brought a couple teammates down with me, they got hooked up and nine months later I got a phone call from Larry Smith saying one of the girls was pregnant but didn't know if it was a bloke or a yank.

And with all that I did, I tried to train the team, even inviting the Wiesbaden team to participate. And I was eternally thankful to Capt. Jahnke, who gave me my freedom, and Lou Boone, who would get things done when I was gone.

In April I went back to NATO, this time to Schiffen, where work continued on the joint document, again a captain's slot. When I arrived I was the only Sgt. on the staff. My boss was a Belgium major from the 2nd Belgium Para Commandos. I was surprised to learn that the 322 Air Division flew combat drops and dropped them in Stanleyville and other points in the Belgium Congo in the 50s and early 60s.

While in conversation over a beer, I brought up my Rope/Pibal/Radar Beacon projects and he became very interested in the Pibal/Radar. I had submitted this idea several times through my own channels any time that I could, but never heard anything back. The paras had been using the fast rope for some time. He was very interested when I explained that the CARP could be defined on the ground and that IFR drops would be permitted. He said he would send the idea up his chain of command. And he also invited me to go climbing the week I was through with my NATO business, at Saint-Etiene, south of Lyon, France, which I jumped at. Again into the gear and up the mountain. It in fact, compared to Norway, was an easy ascension, only for a short space traversing a wall, and no glacier work.

And we received a request from the 322nd Air Division to assist the newly forming South African Army in air drop operations. We found out that in fact, our 22 SAS friends were in charge of the training profile for the newly forming unit. So I called Larry Smith and he gave me the number for their detachment in Pretoria, the Air Division cut orders, I made arrangements and off I went on a six week TDY to teach, and I loved it.

The staff was composed of a conglomeration of nations, mostly Belgians and SAS, I being the only American. The students were to be the cadre for future training of their forces. The quarters and food were in a hotel in Pretoria, and the academic training site was in Salvokop Park, referred to as 'speccop.' By the way, Pretoria was one of the most beautiful cities I had ever seen. There was a tree there, I don't recall the name, that was in blossom throughout the city and it was striking. Very beautiful.

Field training was done 'in the bush' about one hundred miles southwest on the bend of a river, 'Site Charlie,' where amphibious techniques and all of the other 'specialties' were taught. There was a small three thousand foot assault strip and about two dozen Belgian, I was told, Quonset Huts. I, of course, used the strip for LZ and part of a DZ, the Africans had no use for an extraction system. The Africans provided all equipment and air support, including their C-123s and French transports.

The South Africans, since 1965, had been combating a communist organization on the border in southwest Africa. Their effort, as far as aerial delivery was concerned, was resupply and not personnel drop, although that might conceivably happen. They needed a system that would allow them to drop over heavy vegetation and forest up to one hundred feet tall and be recovered quickly so as to not announce the existence of their patrol units. The average bundle would be rations, ammo and support stuff for units continually in the field for six months at a time. The bundles would average about three hundred pounds, mostly ammo and rations. I therefore recommended a drop altitude of eight hundred feet using the British twenty-six foot canopy, with a 125 foot extension line, which the SAS provided.

And if any CCT read this, I taught a ground release point based on a PIBAL, the release point being marked with an X any way possible, VS 17s, trees branches, stamped in snow, mud or sand, or nine troops laying on their bellies. At night marked with lights, and distance and direction broadcast identifying the release point from the IP at six minutes. And to mark the release point, in heavy vegetation or forest, they would launch three PIBAL balloons tethered together, just above the canopy, six minutes from drop. At night it would have two strobe lights per balloon. Using this, the students would get twenty meter impacts eighty percent of the time.

And a nice side benefit. One of the cadre was an Israeli Intelligence Officer belonging to the Mossad, who taught tactical intelligence gathering. Dan (something) who was my roommate and I became close. One night Dan, who was obviously a history buff, told me this story:

"There are three branches of Israeli Intelligence, the Mossad which is like your CIA, Shin Bet, like your FBI and the last which is classified. Mossad and Shin Bet service graduations are held on a plateau called Masada located in the south of Israel on the edge of the desert overlooking the Red Sea. It is a place held in great reverence by all Israeli's, especially the military, because of what happened there."

He continued, "In 73 CE, the Romans had invaded Palestine. As a result, a patriot band, called Jiiean, had formed and occupied the summit, blocking the path of the invading Romans."

"The Romans began construction of an assault ramp up the side of the plateau and when it became apparent the resistance forces could not hold them off, 960 drew lots, each killing another in rotation, until the final survivor, after torching the food warehouse and other structures, killed himself, in violation of strict Israeli religious code. There are varying reports, of survivors, some saying that a women hid herself and her 5 children in a drainage culvert."

He then went on to comment about several other items in past middle eastern history.

And as it so happened my luck ran true to form. When my tour was finished, I was to connect with a Belgium shuttle that would bring me to Nairobi where I would transfer to the Mildenhall shuttle. But Dan had other plans and invited me to Jerusalem to see Masada, thence catching the shuttle from the Air Force base in Tel Aviv. I checked in with Col. Byrd to make sure it was okay and we boarded an Israeli C-130 and flew to the Air Force base at Tel Aviv, then choppered back and saw a Shin Bet graduation. It was a very moving experience, even though conducted in a language I did not understand.

At this point, during commanders call, it was announced, with great fanfare, that T.Sgt. Philip Ward had been promoted to M.Sgt.!

Thence to JTF Deep Furrow, with J-3 duty at Naples Italy with AFSOUTH. More staff work, again subbing for a captain, no problems to speak of. And there was a club there, the Flamingo Club that really jumped. The Italian ladies swamped the club on weekends, at all hours. Most were looking for American husbands, but not all.

I joined up with some Stateside CCT at Kavala, Greece, four days in the field, and worked the drop. And we got a chance to dive off the cliffs for octopus and one of the small restaurants would cook them for us.

Went to the Foreword Air Control School (FAC) at 10th SF Group Bad in Toltz, Germany and while there, I lied about my qualifications and made two HALO jumps from eighteen thousand. I had read that the USMC in fact were using radar beacons with their ANGLICO teams. At FAC School I brought this up and was told it was "being staffed." I always wondered.

In December I was alerted to another J-3 tasking exercise, Lexius, to be held in and around Turkey. It was to be a joint airborne/amphibious exercise with live naval gunfire. This combination of strategic assault really got my attention, but it was cancelled.

And then a problem descended on me. I received a query from AF HQ asking if my wife, Patricia Enzler, who had run up $22,000 in medical bills was authorized to do so. And now, my Mexican divorce came back to haunt me. Legally I was a bigamist, and I could see all kinds of problems developing. That night I went home to Jeannie and explained the situation.

She listened intently and I told her that tomorrow, she needed to go to the squadron commander and complain that I was beating her and the children, maybe with a sniffle or so, and state that she wanted to go home. He was bound by regulation to allow premature rotation in these cases. This would allow them to be out of the theatre safe at home, in case the other shoe should drop.

She did so and the squadron commander issued emergency travel orders authorizing her to return to our home of record, Dexter, Missouri.

Four days later, in the Passenger Terminal, I was standing with Jeannie and the kids, with my arm around her and hers around me, when I felt someone staring at me. I turned and there was the squadron commander, his face slowly turning red and his teeth clenched.

The next day he had me report to him and ate my ass out because I had hoodwinked him. But the family was safe and sound in Dexter, and I never heard another peep from the Air Force.

In Febuary 1969, Tom Saunders relieved me and I was asked to take a new job just created, CCT and Aerial Delivery Training while awaiting my orders to go home, which I did. I took Tom down to 21 SAS in London to introduce him to 'the blokes' and saw, at a distance, Col. David Sterling, very tall and impressive, who had started the SAS in Africa in 1941.

Because of my service to the Regiment, 21 SAS presented me a set of SAS wings "WHO DARES WINS" and one of their sweaters, with the wings on the right upper arm.

And all because of flirting on an airplane.

Lockbourne AFB Columbus, Ohio. Upon arrival I found a nice house for the family and brought them here from Dexter, probably not a moment too soon. Mike had been running wild since McChord, and it had finally caught up with him. He had stolen the mayor's car in Dexter, was arrested and had been sent to a juvenile home.

Here I bought my first love, a Doberman Pincher, whose name, as all of his successors were, was Jake, a seventy pound, fantastic, black and tan animal. I worked and worked with him and in no time he was squared away. He even had started picking up on silent commands.

There was a twenty-four man team there, Larry Lower, Pete Nelson, Maj. John Gillespie, Capt. Holder, Lt. O'Brien, Jim Hardin, Bob Kelly, John Smith and others whose names escapes me. We had two DZs, the Panama operations and what came to be my favorite, the gun range at Camp Atterbury, Indiana. It was just what I wanted. It was, in fact, the Reserve Infantry Training Area for the Indiana National Guard.

It had rappelling towers, gun pits, ambush lanes, rivers and streams. It had classrooms already set to diagram demo and small unit tactics. The Range Master was Mr. Dyes, a retired TAC Lt. Col. fighter pilot, who loved to rappel with us, unofficially of course.

At Camp Atterbury was the gun range for our spooks, the AC13's. These were in essence, airborne artillery, having two action express fifty caliber machine guns and a 155 howitzer installed firing from the left side of the aircraft. The CP was 200 yards from the target area, several old busses and cars.

Almost immediately after my arrival we began RECONDO style training there, and most importantly Mr. Dyes was able to provide blank .223 ammo. And here is where Steve, my son, picked up some wonderful memories. As often as not I took him to Atterbury where I treated him as just another controller. Even letting him carry an M-16, loaded naturally with blanks. But he rappelled with us, went on patrol, set ambushes and had a hell of a time.

My favorite memory. The AC-130 Squadron called me one day and said that next week, the secretary of the AF was going to visit the mission. Was there anything we could do to make his experience memorable? I said, in fact there was, I would make some arrangements and advice. I went to Mr. Dyes and explained that I would like the base engineers to provide us with a fifty-five gal drum half full of gasoline, four pounds of C-4 and an electric detonator run back to our CP. He agreed and I briefed the spooks. They thought my plan was great.

On the night in question, spook called in six minutes out, I replied he was cleared to fire. As he started. I twisted the handle and the C-4 ignited, throwing a huge fireball into the sky. Not only was the SecAF impressed, he was thrown around. I found out later that rather than firing from 1200 feet, they had dropped down to 800 for a closer look. In any event Lockbourne was a lot of fun.

And a glorious trip. I had been in Panama for a couple weeks and it was time to fly home on the commuter C-130. This bird flew out of Lockbourne once a week to Panama and any embassy in South America that had need of the courier service. I decided to catch the bird on the way into South America instead of when he was coming back, just for the hell of it. So we hit Brasilia, for two days. And as we were approaching Rio de Janerio, the number four engine failed. It was a bad carburetor and we found that it would take a week or so to get it repaired so we all journeyed downtown to a hotel. And the party started!

And visited, wow! Ipanema Beach with the lovely almost nothing bathing suits, the bay, Pedro De Arpoder with the Sugarloaf Mountain, and most impressive, the statue of Cristo Redentor overlooking Rio, one hundred feet tall and one of the new seven wonders of the world. The view of Rio from the foot of the statue was breathtaking! And on the way back, Buenos Aires and Lima, Peru, one day in each. The lady in Rio was super! A thoroughly delightful trip!

Except that here was my only exposure to a combat controller that was an asshole, I do not remember his name.

I had a party at my house for Jeannie and one of the controllers who had the same birthday. Of course there was a lot of drinking, dancing, etc. About ten, in came this guy and three controllers, all a little drunk. They started with the bad language, one of them, feeling one of the girlfriends up and then insulting my wife. So I told them to leave which they did.

The next morning after formation I told him to stand fast, and, after everyone left, I took off my shirt and told him, to, take his best shot. He stood there, I pushed his chest, screamed at him, and called him a chicken shit (expletive). Instead he said he wanted to apologize to me and the others. We shook hands. As far as I know no one on the team was aware what happened.

About this time, Mike enlisted in the Army and was sent to Ft. Knox for AIT.

By coincidence, we were tasked to send a Training Team there to teach an Army H-21 unit how to rappel, because they were alerted to deploy to Nam and time was very short. Why us, I never was able to determine.

I took Smitty and two others and off we went .Upon arrival, I decided to visit Mike at his training company and when I walked into the company HQ, here was my son standing at parade rest next to an old stove. The 1st Sgt. explained that he was fighting in the barracks. We decided an Article Fifteen was not the answer so Mike did four weeks of extra detail.

He then went to Nam as a door gunner and upon return got in serious trouble. But back to the helicopters.

We had a class of about fifteen, and located some cliffs near the post, which we used for basic training. After four days, they seemed comfortable with the procedure, so we rigged a doughnut ring, the carabiner anchor point, on one of the birds, launched it and they all made three rappels from sixty feet. Strangely, for entry in their records they could not be trained for rappelling unless it was by an Army unit, so I told them to annotate 'abseiling,' which is the German term. The last night, we went to the club and I got hammered. Driving to our motel, I could not find first gear and rolled back, twice into the front of a patrol car. I spent that night in the slammer, and paid a $300 fine the next morning.

But one final story, to show the dark side of a combat controller. The names are fictitious because if they are still alive, I do not want to cause them problems. I was sitting at my desk one day and the phone rang. On it was a police Sgt. asking if John Brown was available. I replied that Sgt. Brown was TDY and would be gone awhile and I asked if there was a problem. The officer stated, in a hushed voice, that John's wife had been raped and she was in the hospital. I told him I would get John back ASAP and send some help to his wife, Mary.

I immediately made arraignments to recover John, and when he asked, I replied that there was a problem here. I then called my wife and briefed her. She said she would contact the wives and arrange for them to be with Mary, twenty-four hours a day.

John arrived the next day and I met him at planeside. I briefed him and he hopped in and I drove him home to pick up his car. And a word about John. He was a quiet, somewhat withdrawn, thin young man, who looked you in the eye when he talked with you, and took his duties very seriously. His performance evaluations were above normal but not outstanding. He and Mary had been married about 4 years and had one daughter, Prisie. I told him to take off and be gone as long as he needed, it was not necessary for him to apply for any leave.

Two weeks later John showed up. Mary was recovering nicely and apparently had not been impregnated. The wives had worked it out so if John was at work, one of them would be with Mary. He said that the police had two suspects, one a shoe salesman and the other a grocery clerk, but they had no proof.

A couple months went by and one day I asked how the investigation was going. John shrugged and said, "Nowhere." He said he was checking a few things out himself. I told him if he needed any help, to let me know. With that he thanked me and turned away.

Six months passed, as they do, and life continued with its variances. I sent John off on a TDY where he would work by himself for two weeks or so, a week passed and I received a call from the same Sgt. who I had talked to originally. He again asked if John was available, and I again replied that he was TDY, and asked the same question, any problems? There was a short pause and he said, "Two nights ago we found the grocery clerk dead in an alley with his throat cut." And he asked me, "Are you sure John is TDY"? And I said, of course. But we knew.

No one on the Team, including John, ever brought it up again. By its silence the Team stood up for one of their own. Chief Howell came in and relieved me and I retired in June 1971 returning to Dexter, Missouri.

Change of Uniforms

The family, including Jake, returned to Dexter because Jeannie convinced me. Her Uncle was a major player and we could have a very successful life there in that small town. Upon arrival of course there were reunions and introductions and 'getting to know yous.' Most importantly, a reunion with her mom and dad, Gladys and Ab, who owned a very successful dump truck business. They were just country folk, but very fine ones.

I met her Uncle, who owned the local lumber yard and a bowling alley and although he was a little withdrawn, offered to check around and see what was available. In the meantime, he had arraigned for us to rent a small farm, complete with barn and horse. Waiting for our furniture, we stayed with Ab and Gladys. It was crowded but warm and friendly. Ab and I talked about me coming in with him, but he didn't think there was enough work to keep two trucks busy.

Although I never considered myself a salesman, I found a job selling mobile homes for a Cousin of Jeannie's, or her Uncle had actually arraigned it. It was a small salary plus commission located next to her cousins real estate office. And Jeannie told me why her Uncle was a little short with me.

Jeannie had met Dave, her first husband, while Dave was going through preflight training at a small Air Force base in Mauldin, Missouri, down the road apiece. They, in fact, had met at a dance on base, dated while he was in school, and married when he graduated. A classmate of Dave's, at the same time, was dating her Uncle's daughter, Joyce. They were also married and at the end of his tour. He got out, returning to Dexter to manage the bowling alley. Dave and the Uncle had developed a very close bond, and when Jeannie divorced him, the Uncle took it personally and tried very hard to dissuade her. I was not his favorite guy.

Off to work wearing a tie, settling in the office with my eyes on the lot, waiting for an 'up,' and waiting, and waiting. There were probably about two or three lookers every day, Saturdays, perhaps four. I believe I was there for about three weeks before I sold my first unit, and collected by first commission, eight hundred. And lo and behold, the next week another unit and another commission seven hundred fifty. Hell maybe this was going to work, after all. And about this time I made friends with one of the Dexter police officers, John Netter, who had served with the 173rd Airborne Infantry in Nam.

And three the doors one morning came an attractive thirty-year-old lady, jeans and a tight tank top. She had purchased a mobile home several months ago from the real estate owner, and was having a problem, she thought, with the plumbing.

Would I come out and take a look at it? YOU BETCHA!

The next day at about ten A.M. I closed the lot and went over to her unit, located on the outskirts of Dexter, on a small lot clustered with trees. She opened the door, batted her blue eyes and invited me in, introducing herself as Lucy and we shook hands. She asked me if I would like a cup of coffee, which I of course accepted. I asked her what her plumbing problem was and she said the hot water heater did not seem to heat up properly, but she had turned it up and it was okay now, smiling at me. We chatted for a while and Lucy explained that her husband was a truck driver and gone a lot. I finished my coffee and as I left, with a wink, I told her if she needed anything else fixed, to call me. HOT DOG!

Two days later, she did, we skipped the coffee and headed right for bed. She was outstanding, and our affair continued while I was in Dexter, about five months.

Back on the farm everyone seemed content. Occasionally I would get a letter from Mike and he would relate his tales of derring-do in country. Jake and I romped in the front yard, and he was getting smarter by the day. He would lay under the one tree we had, and watch the occasional car go by, waiting for me to come home. I had him trained not to leave the yard, regardless of the temptation or provocation. Occasionally I would go saddle the horse and off we would go, at a slow pace, traveling the dirt roads surrounding the farm. Jake trotting along by our side. And once and awhile we would go bowling with Joyce and her husband, for free! And occasionally, square dancing on Saturday night at the VFW Club.

But I was getting edgy. The small town gatherings were a bore. The conversation was of wheat, hogs, and late-blooming flowers. I did not like my job, or most people I knew. I realized I was having a hard time adjusting to the civilian environment. Uncle's idea of being a gracious host, was a nod when you came in the door.

One afternoon when I arrived home after work Jeannie said that she had not seen Jake for some time. My heart immediately skipped a beat, and we all set out to find him, first on the grounds and then we fanned out from the house. Steve, by the side of the road, about one hundred feet down from the driveway, shouted and then dropped down on his knees. I ran to him and there was Jake, dead in a culvert, the victim of a passing motorist.

Steve was crying and it hit me like a kick in the stomach. I carried Jake back to the house in my arms and that night we carefully and lovingly delivered his eulogy burying him under the tree he liked so much. The next day I found a dobie Pup and brought her home. Her name, like all of the others for the next forty years, and there were six of them, was named Jake.

One night, really restless, after work, I went down to the local honky-tonk and got completely blitzed. At closing somehow I managed to drive home, and got the car parked relatively straight. Staggered in the house, with everyone asleep, got undressed in the bathroom, took my 1911, a .45 caliber pistol, out of the desk drawer and hollered out in a fit of rage, "ANYONE(EXPLETIVE)WHO COMES IN IS GONNA DIE!" That woke Jeannie and she and the children fled to the kitchen, blocking the door with the table, where Jeannie called the police officer friend of mine, John and begged for help.

I had passed out, John told me later and the pistol and fallen from my grip .I was slumped against the shower wall. He took the 1911, and he and Jeannie carried me into the bedroom, throwing me on the bed. He stayed in the kitchen with Jeannie all night and the next morning, when I started to come around. He told me what I had said and done. I could remember nothing. For the second time in my life, I was ashamed of something I had done. I apologized to Jeannie and the children profusely and also to John, who delivered a stern warning, one GI to the other.

Next day I went to work, still bothered and upset. I was finding fault with everything and everybody. Days pasted without a sale. In fact not even lookers. Lucy showed up one day and quietly asked why I had not been around and I told her I had not been feeling well. Finally I sold one, but the bank turned down the financing.

That night I came home and told Jeannie to start packing, we were going back to Sacramento. The next week the movers showed, packed our stuff and off we went to California.

Upon arrival, we found a small house and rented it. Close friends of Jeannie's, Carla and Jerry Ludwigson showed up and welcomed us back to Sacramento. Jerry had been Dave's flight engineer for several years, and all four had become close. I asked Jerry if he knew of any work, and he immediately responded that the base bowling alley that he managed, was short a soda jerk. I said, "Why not? Until I can find something better."

As it happened, I stayed there for about four months, got lucky and was serviced by one of the customers several times in the parking lot. Jeannie had taken a job at a department store to help make ends meet.

One day, I stumbled on a want ad that advertised for a security manager. I responded, the interview being in San Francisco by the outgoing West Coast VP, and I was hired. The job was as his replacement, the Western VP for operations for Hargrave Security and Investigative Bureau, a nationwide firm, with six offices in California that I would be responsible for, and the salary was double what I was making. They had no problem moving corporate to Sacramento, I came home and danced a jig, Jeannie was absolutely thrilled. I told her she could quit her job, but she said she enjoyed it, and would like to continue.

And life shifted into high gear. I activated my GI Bill. Registered at Sacramento State College in August of 1972 majoring, naturally, in criminal justice. Every Monday morning, at seven A.M., I would leave for work, close up shop at five, and head over for my first class on campus, and end the last class at ten P.M. That was the schedule Monday through Friday for four long years. I then registered for the masters program, wrote my thesis "Nuclear Terrorism" but after six months the

GI Bill ran out so I quit. The weekends I tried to reserve only for the family, and we tried to do something with Jake and the kids.

From this point on, as a break, I have included the occasional PI story in *this type of print.*

One morning, my secretary told me that an ex-employee was on the line and wanted to talk to the boss. I picked up the phone and he said he had worked for Hargraves a couple years ago, I asked him for his name and he refused, so I asked him what he wanted. He said he worked in a restaurant in Modesto with a guy named Simmons who had killed a cop in San Bernardino two years ago. I reached over and quickly turned on the phone recorder. I had him repeat it and he did. I asked why he didn't' go to the cops there and he said he was afraid the guy would find out and kill him, too. I asked for all of the information he had and he had little, other than to say that this guy was coming to Sacramento in two days (Thursday) to attend his mother's funeral at one P.M. He thought it was the funeral home on Greenback Lane but wasn't sure. We talked a bit more but he had nothing more to add. I asked for his number and he refused and hung up. I put up a reverse check on the call and found it came from a pay phone.

I grabbed the recorder and presented myself at the Sheriff's Office. I explained to the desk Sgt. what I had and he escorted me to Homicide where I met Sgt. John Slaybaugh. I told him what I had and turned on the recorder. As soon as he heard where the officer was killed, he jumped up excitedly and said he knew about this case. By this time several detec-

tives were clustered around, listening intently and taking notes. He thanked me and ask if he could have the tape and I said certainly. I asked him to call me when something happened. He promised he would.

I went back to work, and when I came in Thursday, I was really attuned to the telephone. Noon and no call, three P.M. and no call, five P.M. and nothing. So the next morning I went back to see Sgt. Slaybaugh. Very sheepishly he admitted they had the funeral grounds surrounded and saw him enter. And then they lost him. But to his credit, a couple weeks later he called me and said that Simmons had been arrested in Modesto, at the restaurant. I thanked him and from then on I had a friend in the Sheriff's department.

My income had drastically improved and we had a few dollars in savings, so we bought a two story home in Citrus Heights, a Sacramento suburb. In fact, it was the Ludwigson's who had alerted us, it being right across the street from them. And an additional benefit from Jerry and Carla. They had a daughter, Lynn, who was an accomplished artist and she did a charcoal sketch of Jake which presently hangs in my grandson's bedroom. Our house was nice, but a little small in the living room, so I had an idea, I closed off the garage and made it into the family room, complete with card table and a bar. Plenty of good times ensued.

But Jeannie again was becoming different. We eventually reached the point where I was not happy with her. We would argue and she would pout, not speaking for days. I would be grumpy and self-centered. I thought that if we were able to participate in something together, it would help, so we began to play tennis together, but that died quickly. Our sex life wasn't one.

Steve was now seventeen and a handful to deal with. Cathy turned sixteen and her interest in boys accelerated, culminating in me knocking on her boyfriend's door at two A.M. issuing a stern warning, and bringing her home. Steve decided to leave home, 'borrowed' a car and ended up in Kansas. Susan, who was always my favorite, and Jimmy were super.

And I, of course, was on the prowl and found a classmate that satisfied my urges.

Next door lived Pat and Jennette Barker and their three children, Rei was sixteen, Ray fourteen, and Lara nine. Pat worked at the local newspaper, and Jennette was a stunning woman. From the very first introduction across our backyard fence, I was captivated. She was slim, with a good build and had a Louisiana drawl. At first I was not sexually drawn to her, but I was certainly emotionally captured. We became friends with them, occasionally going to Reno and doing a little gambling.

We received notification that Ab, Jeannie's father, had suffered a heart attack and had died, so Jeannie flew back for the funeral and I baby sat. It was work, travel to the sub offices every couple months, do some investigations, head for classes and try and stay level and on track. And with my luck, I ended up on the Dean's List.

In 1976, I got my degree and my private investigators license in the same month, and started my career. And I had applied for every course that the California Department of Justice had, and for almost nine more months I went to school again at night. And completed, the criminal investigators course, fraud and asset identification, background checks, search and seizure, the California penal code, legal research and a few others. I was accepted as an investigator for both the Sacramento and Yuba County Public Defender's Offices. I got off to a pretty fast start, within the first three months I worked a murder in Camptonville, California involving the ambush killing of a police officer by an indigent, Zane Caldwell, followed by a women who was murdered in an alley by her husband, Cory Schroder.

One day a lady in Camptonville peered out of her window and saw young man, naked, in the front window on the second story of a house across the street. She called the police and a CHP Officer, Don Brown responded. Officer Brown entered and the witness stated that several minutes later she heard two shots. Other officers responding stated that apparently Officer Brown had confronted Caldwell who fired two shots from his shotgun killing the officer. A drug test on Caldwell tested positive for cocaine.

This was my initial assignment from the Yuba County office. I had heard that the DA's investigator had visited the witness several times. It made me wonder why more than perhaps, twice. I interviewed her and found that the DA had conducted four interviews with her, asking different questions.

On a hunch, I asked her if they had given her a copy, of the first interview, she replied they had and I asked if I could make a copy of those documents. She okayed that and I ran down to the local print shop and had it done. Upon examination it was obvious that she had given the investigator different stories and he had tried to correct her. At trial, her candor was questioned but to no avail. Caldwell was found guilty.

Corey Schroder, bartender and minor drug dealer had gotten in an argument with his wife one night, they had gone outside the bar and in a rage, he cut her throat. One night I had finished interviewing a witness and walked to my car. As I opened my car door, a shot rang out and heard a ping. I ducked down, drew my weapon and tried to locate the origin of the shot, but couldn't. I waited several minutes, becoming attuned to my surroundings. Nothing happened, so I cautiously stood up. There was a bullet hole in my fender, just in front of the driver's door. My hourly rate just increased.

In the course of wandering around Marysville, the location of the bar, I had met some drug dealers. And I now learned that the cartel was concerned about my snooping because they thought the investigation was drug orientated. I assured them that the drug trafficking was no concern of mine. In this case, like Caldwell, the defendant was found guilty.

But the business slackened as the PI business does, so I looked around for a job and went to work for Radio Shack. In fact, this would become my modus operandi for the rest of my investigator career. My first love was investigations, but often the well was dry and I would work elsewhere, simultaneously on occasion, if I could arrange it.

And our neighbor Jennette and I were drawing closer by the day, although there were no outward signs. We had not talked of any possibilities, but there were long glances and the warmth was there. Occasionally, as friends do, I would steal a hug or perhaps hold her hand. And it was becoming apparent that her marriage to Pat was rocky.

One afternoon, there was a knock on the front door, I opened it and there stood Gladys, with two suitcases. I was stunned! I brought her and her bags in and asked her what was up? She replied that she had come to live with us! I made her comfortable and tried to be friendly and considerate, seeing as how she was a recent widow but...

When Jeannie got home I took her in the bedroom and shouted, "What the hell is going on?" She said that her mother had sold her house and come to live with us!

I hit the roof, asking why she had not asked me, or at least mentioned it and she replied she didn't think I would care. At that point the marriage died and I moved into an apartment that week. That caused many casualties, Jake was one of them. I could not keep him, and Jeannie was not interested, so I found a friendly farmer who adopted her. I heard several years later he had died of cancer.

And my social life once again accelerated. I became intimate with another apartment dweller, a waitress in Folsom, where I managed a Radio Shack store, and my relationship with Jennette took off. Coincidently, she and Pat had come to a parting of the ways and he had moved out. Jennette and I had never been intimate and I was not involved in any way with Pat's decision.

And I thought it was time for me to get out of the apartment, with all of the distractions, and presuming I would be a bachelor for some time, I bought a mobile home in a park.

And one day, I got a shock. I received a phone call from Donald and David, who were in the Navy and wanted to visit, and I of course said come on by. David showed up, and Jan and I took him to Reno where he promptly lost fifty dollars at the blackjack table. I, by coincidence, had been studying an Australian card counting system and had been reasonably successful at the tables. It only worked with single deck and then only made the odds even, instead of stacked to the house. At this time, there were still a few single deck houses left, and we happened to be in one of them. I took him, and within fifteen minutes, with a ten dollar bank, got his money back, stood up and left the tables.

Jan had seen me do that several times and was not surprised. David was dumbfounded. He started in excitedly explaining why I should continue, and as I had explained to Jan, this 'system' could only be used sometimes and only made the odds even. It did not guarantee I would win always. In my opinion people who visit the gaming tables with the intent of beating the house are fools. Those who play for entertainment are one group, those who risk a house payment or food on the table are another.

And at this point I began getting strange phone calls. Every three or four days, I would receive a phone call from a young girl, I would suspect between ten and twelve, who kept asking me if I wanted a date. The first couple times I just laughed and hung up. But about the third I asked her to identify herself and she refused, and the eighth time, I agreed and asked her to come to the mobile home, so I could alert her parents, and that ended that. I always had the opinion it was one of Lara's little girlfriends and they had decided to pull a trick on me.

And I decided that it was time for me to satisfy one of my urges, so I went to a boat show and bought a really neat twenty-two foot Catalina sailboat. Jan and I took it out to Lake Folsom, a nearby recreation area, and launched it in a six knot breeze.

Of course I had no sailing lessons, so the first hour was a lot of running into the dock and beach, but I finally got it figured out, realizing the pressure differential on either side of the sail was just like an aircraft's wings, and off we went, zipping along.

And for several seasons that little boat provided our main entertainment. I modified a few things, a radio with twin stereo speakers, racks in the cockpit so we could sleep outside at night, and odds and ends. Eventually I got Jan and Ray checked out and we spent many enjoyable days and nights aboard. We sailed up both of the rivers feeding the lake, and camped on a number of shores and inlets, once taking it down south and sailing San Francisco Bay for a few days.

Unfortunately, Sacramento, and the rest of California went through an extended drought season where the water level was too low to sail, so I sold the boat.

And again hitting a slack time, I went to work at the Rancho Seco Nuclear Plant as part of their Security Force. If I passed probation, I was told they would promote me immediately to a supervisor. I passed my probation but was instead promoted to the training officer, responsible for seventy officers and their compliance with the Sacramento Sheriff's Office and the NRC rules and regulations. I was sent to Denver, Colorado to the NRC Schools and completed the following courses, site security, defensive tactics for a nuclear site, contamination force protection and counter terrorist operations, several others, and this is of course is what I in turn taught the force.

One day several weeks after Pat had left, and I had been in the park for a two months or so, Jennette came to visit and the spark was fully ignited. I told her I loved her and wanted to marry her. It was more fulfilling and wonderful than any other experience I had. And she said yes. Maybe for the first time in my life, I had fallen deeply in love. I believe that was the actual beginning of my final transitional turn. I stopped smoking and more importantly drinking, and even more important than that, I was never unfaithful again. Years later, as I write this, it has been thirty-seven years of marriage, mostly good times, a few bad, but I have never strayed, or for that matter never considered it, which constantly has me in awe.

And so I moved in with her and her children, and we were married December 8th, 1980. And throughout, every winter we would go to Heavenly Valley or Boreal Ridge and ski, at least twice a month. We had a blast, and in the process I taught Ray and Lara how and they both loved it. In fact, we spent our seven day honeymoon at Boreal in the apartments they leased, skiing in the day and loving during the night.

Closer to the Top

One morning I received a phone call from an attorney who said that he had a client who was female and black. She had attempted to rent an apartment in an upper class area and had been refused. He wanted to know if I thought we could do something about this, admitting he had no ideas on how to approach it. My response was to 'go for the throat' and I asked him for the particulars.

I briefed Jennette, who I recruited, and not for the first time. We would visit the Manager and she was to accelerate her drawl. I would tell the Manager that I was exploring new sales territory for our business in Louisiana. I traveled a lot, and I was concerned about the 'environment' I would leave her in. She grinned and said, "let's play."

As we entered his office, the Manager rose and greeted us. I explained what was up, and with a raised eyebrow, explained that I was concerned about the " environment" I would be leaving my wife in. He assured me that this was an *upscale complex and they had "strict rules about tenants." I asked who is and who is not allowed? With a knowing smile he said, "Don't worry sir, we don't rent to mexes or niggers."*

I appeared skeptical and quizzical. He said, "Wait a minute and I'll prove it." And disappeared into his back office. In a moment he returned and said, "These are my instructions from corporate , you can have a copy if you want." I scanned the document and said, "Yeah, I'd like a copy." He produced it, I told him a representative would return to make the arrangements and we took it to the attorney.

On the second page was an admonition that "no applicant who is not white will be accepted." The attorney grinned and bought both Jan and I lunch aboard the Delta Queen, an exclusive restaurant aboard an old paddle wheeler, docked on the Sacramento River. The client, I understood, a year later, settled out of court for six figures.

I found a job with a small appliance dealer to learn the repair business. He had a friend, Buss Martin, who was also a repairman with tons of experience. They would do joint ventures occasionally if the job was too big for just one of them.

After six months of learning the craft, I had an idea. I told Jan I would like to go into the appliance repair, rental, and sales business. We had a pickup with a lift gate. I would have to buy some special equipment such as regulators, welding unit and the like but the total outlay would be no more than $500. As far as I knew, there was no one renting appliances except new ones, which were pretty pricey. I had done some research and thought we could buy an old appliance, repair it and rent it for eighteen dollars per month, and after four months we should recoup our expenses. And we could market the ones in excellent condition, guaranteed, for half of what a new one would be. There should also be some repair business. She excitedly agreed.

So I did more research and built a business plan. I also contacted Buss to see if he was hirable and he was. So we started with a small inexpensive ad working out of our (Jennette's) garage. The ad to purchase was published Friday afternoon. Saturday, no calls, Sunday, no calls, but Monday afternoon the phone started to ring. By the end of the first week we had washers and dryers, most of which we either paid five dollars for or hauled off for free. These were what I perceived we would rent. They were piled in the backyard and Buss and I were working sixteen hours a day to get them ready. A month later we had nine pairs, one set retail ready. And I placed an ad in the Pennysaver, an inexpensive want ad flyer. In four days all of the units were rented.

Next month was a repeat. I hired Mike, my son, who had recently arrived from Idaho, to pick up and deliver. Buss and I continued all out. All told, at this point I was $4,000 in debit. In bed one night I told Jan I thought it was time to make a move, she agreed and within a week I had rented a store for $600 a month plus utilities in downtown Roseville, a small town on the north edge of Sacramento.

In November 1981, PJ Appliance was born. The store was ideal. It had a forty-foot frontage, twenty feet deep, just right for a sales floor and behind the back wall was a space for a triple car garage. It had, in fact been an auto repair business a couple years prior. There was even a small office on the back wall. We hired a second trainee repairman. Jan's son Ray.

During the day, we worked like dogs, and in the evening, I did the remodeling that was necessary. I was now $6,000 in debt.

My business plan called for us to break even in the sixth month and, at that point, we were in fact, about $1,200 ahead. But I was not taking any wages, it was all going to the hired help. We had grown to four technicians and another pickup truck for repairs, and a technician to do them. Any thought of the PI business was put on hold.

The paper work and appointment setting, the scheduling of both trucks and acquiring of parts that we had not stripped off the unrepairable units was too much for me, and Buss told me his wife was available and I hired her as my secretary and gopher.

She became a godsend. She did all of the posting, set all appointments, talked to the occasional retail customer and did the parts run. I covered the store on weekends.

My bookkeeper and I checked the GNA and for the seventh month, our total expenses were $8,040 and we had 412 units out on rental at eighteen dollars each for $7,500 and twenty-four sales for an average of eighty-five dollars each, $2,000, sixteen repair jobs for $1,900 all for a total net of $3,300 but probably about $2,200. Not bad but not good enough to keep me from worrying.

And a story. One Sunday a guy came in and I sold him a dryer. He gave me his address and I said I would deliver it when I closed that day. I drove to Rocklin, knocked on the door, and Susie opened the door, saw me and went into shock. I smiled, explaining her husband had bought a dryer and she let me in and I began setting it up. And she watched from the doorway, almost in tears. I looked up and said, "Hi Susie, how ya been? No I won't say anything," with that she relaxed and left the doorway. Being replaced by her husband. He and I chatted while I finished up, I shook hands and left.

While I was at Travis, Susie worked in the NCO club and augmented her income with trips to the parking lot, a couple times to my Fiat, with the top up.

The second year Jan, Lara, and I went to Hawaii and stayed for two glorious weeks. And on top of that, Pat started making noises about selling their house, so we looked around and bought a house in Citrus Heights about three miles away. A very nice one story home with a large back yard, only about eight years old.

So in the midst of running the business and Jan, at this point working full time for Kaiser, we squeezed in the move, at one point bringing the last load of furniture over at two A.M. Rei had found romantic interests and had moved out. Ray would not be far behind her.

I was hired by a club owner to see if one of his bartender was 'skimming.' So I sat at the bar between the two cash registers. I had talked to the bartender several times, and had told him I was there to watch the ballgame. I got up to go to the bathroom and when I returned there was a guy sitting on my stool. I politely pointed out my drink in front of him and asked him if he would mind moving. He got really stupid in a hurry, turning toward me trying to hit me. It glanced off my shoulder and I introduced him to Mr. Shuto, across the throat and he gasped and slid off the stool and I kicked him in the face. The bartender came around the corner with a billy club in his hand and broke it up.

I regained my seat and the bartender and I got involved in conversation. He was also an ex-GI, Navy, so we had some common ground. He offered to buy me a drink and I declined asking him how he could afford it on a bartenders pay. With a smile he winked at me and said, "Because I take an extra two hundred out of the boss's pocket every night."

Anyway, time went by and I was spending eighty hours a week at the shop and neglecting my home life. Some months I would make a little, some months not. And we were starting to see competition in the rental market. But at the end of the third year, one night, I did not come home and January, at four in the morning, found me asleep on the concrete, in the middle of repairing a refrigerator. I was exhausted, had trouble sleeping and my hands were starting to tremble. The next weekend we had a long talk and I decided to sell the business. I was fortunate and found a buyer, a middle eastern gentleman.

I warned him that this was an honest business, and thirty percent of our income came from property management companies who expected a fair shake. He promised me that would continue, gave me a down payment and I took a quick claim on a condo he owned for the rest.

The fourth month I started to get calls from the property managers complaining that he was double billing, charging for undone repairs and his work was poor. I contacted him, explained what I had heard, and reminded him, how much his unpaid loan to me was.

Seven months later he went out of business, but luckily he had paid off his loan.

An attorney friend invited me to lunch and over it presented his problem. He was involved in a large civil action involving misuse of a county water system The crux was that the company denied any forewarning of a disastrous leak that essentially ruined a number of farms in the surrounding area. The attorney had the court issue a subpoena for the main maintenance supervisor who was still employed by the water company. Information had surfaced that two years ago, he had complained of a valve structure being deficient and was told by his supervisors not to pay any attention to it. His log reflecting that event was 'missing,' Several attempts had been made, but he was obviously dodging service. The prelim was due to start next week.

I went to a local Pizza Hut in my grandson's old pickup truck, bought a pizza hat and a pizza box and headed to his house. Knocked on his door, saw the curtain move and knocked again. A voice from inside said, "What do you want?" I told him I had his pizza. He replied that he had not ordered one. I said, "Look man, this is my last delivery and I got a hot date...do me a favor and just take the pizza, I won't even charge you for it." He opened the door, and I delivered the pizza. The subpoena was in the pizza box.

I thought about going back into Federal Service so that my retirement would increase and so I went to work in the West Sacramento Postal Distribution Center. A year later I was promoted to supervisor and my pay check looked cool.

Meanwhile, Jan and I were talking about moving closer to our work. The house was becoming too big. On weekends Jan would clean and my time was spent doing yard work and maintenance. And the commuting traffic was slowly getting ridiculous. To go fifteen miles, coming or going, it would often take us a half-hour. Ray had left, and Lara would not be far behind him.

So we sold our house and bought a four bedroom condo, one mile from both of our jobs. And it was, and is, a great place to live. The neighborhood was quiet and centrally located and it offered all of the amenities. To put the icing on the cake, we journeyed out and found another Doberman, whose name, of course, became Jake.

This was a male and about seven weeks when we brought him home. That surprised me because of his size, I thought a year. At least. But I jumped right in and began training him. Housebreaking was never a problem. The normal commands, sit, stay, and come he snapped up in a hurry. Arm and hand, or silent commands took several months, but being very familiar with the breed, I understood that. On our first visit to PetSmart, the vet asked me if I knew what I had? I shook my head and he said that Jake was a gladiator.

Dobermans have four sizes, a distinct breed subdivision. And according to size, they were, mini, seven pounds, standard seventy, king one hundred, and gladiator, the largest, sometimes going to 140 pounds. Two years later, full grown, Jake weighed one hundred thirty pounds, a BIG dobie! He was a little on the aggressive side, and as with most of that breed, very protective. I would playfully grab Jan and he would snarl at me. He did not like other pets, and when someone came into the house and sat, Jake had a disconcerting habit of sitting at their feet about two feet away, and, because of his size, staring at them, level, right in the eyes. He made people nervous, so normally, unless the person knew him, he ended up in the garage. And unless provoked, rarely barked, but when he did it got your attention.

Jan and I would occasionally take him for a run in the park. And normally there were 4 or five bums, half-drunk, just hanging. On one of my runs, as I passed by, one of them said, "Nice looking dog, does he bite?" I thought about Jan with Jake running past the same group, and I responded, "Only if I say the magic word." He asked, "And then what?" I replied, "Then he tears your balls off!" Jan reported that when she and Jake were next out, as they approached the group, they got up and moved inside the fenced tennis court, and shut the gate.

The Kaczyniski Affair

Another phone call from a lawyer who I had worked with for some time. His client was a women recently divorced who had been awarded their Cadillac as part of the property settlement. The husband, who she was afraid of, had been in jail several times and refused to turn over the car, which was his favorite. She knew where he used to work, had a spare set of keys, but did not know where the Cadillac was. I had her fill out a questionnaire I had designed which listed numerous possibilities for persons who had disappeared. She had little information other than he was an avid bowler and been doing so for years. And he was a voting registered Democrat.

So I contacted his place of employment and was told he no longer worked there, and did not know where he was at. I called the American Bowling Congress and they had an address, but it was old. I then contacted a friend in voter registration and lo and behold, there was his address, an apartment complex in west Sacramento.

I got hold of my partner, Jan. We were to drive to his address, at two A.M. If the car was there, I would take it and drop it at the airport, in short term parking, where the wife could pick it up. I did not want to take any chances delivering the car to her or to the attorney's office. My wife would follow and pick me up.

We drove by and the car was there so we parked up the street. I got out and quietly approached and when I peered into the window, I could see a teenage girl curled up in the back seat. I stopped and turned around, rejoined Jan and home we went. The next morning called the attorney, before I went to work and told him what occurred and said kidnapping was not my bag. That ended that.

In 1987 I went to work for the USPO at their Processing facility and in a short time, I was promoted to temporary supervisor and then a couple months later, became a real one. Between Jan's salary, my retirement and the post office, we were living well. My first step was to pay off all of our credit cards and throw them in the trash. Next, I insured that our investments, which I had quietly started in 1971, were converted to equities and stabilized.

One day, I was looking at Jake and wondered if I could carve him out of wood. I got a Dremel set and a piece of carving wood, basswood, and started to experiment. I made some mistakes but eventually understood the process and I was hooked.

Every chance I had, I carved. I bought several sets of eyes at the taxidermy and experimented with those, now to mount them. I discovered wood filler that had excellent bonding and filler qualities. I also found that taking a picture, profile, and full faced, would allow me to maintain a true dimension.

After the first six months or so, Jan and I would take them around to various Doberman meets, and amazingly, they sold. And in 1998 I entered the All California wood carving contest and won third in my class. Of course there were only three of us competing but I felt vindicated.

Early in 1994, as I was coming to work wearing my CCT cap, the plant manager, Bob Williamson, was also arriving, glanced at my hat and said, "Combat Control Huh?" I said yeah and we sat down and had a chat. He had been a radio man/teletype operator in the Army, 173rd Airborne Brigade, with a tour in Nam. We chatted for a while, me filing him in on what I had been doing, especially the investigations, which I was still of course, doing on occasion.

A couple months past and one day I was asked to come to his office. Upon arrival I met the West Regional Vice President and they asked me to get comfortable.

The VP asked if I was familiar with the 'Unabomber' situation. Of course I had heard of him. He had been sending bombs through the mail and at this point killed six people and wounded a few others. The VP continued. The airlines had delivered an edict. If one more bomb was found to have been flown on the aircraft, they would no longer fly the mail, in essence curtailing all mail deliveries, everywhere. HQ had decided, because the West Coast was apparently where he had started, they would be tasked with formulating a plan to closely inspect suspect packages.

At this point Bob took over. The reason this facility was tasked was because he dropped one off here, and the clerk was able to provide guidance on his appearance. From this, emerged the famous sketch of the man with the beard and sunglasses, with a hood over his head, subsequently identified as Ted Kaczyniski.

Bob looked at me and said that he had researched my "background "and did I think such an operation could be constructed. I asked if the packages had any identifying characteristics and he said they did. I asked how long did I have and replied with a grimace, one week, and handed me the FBI report which contained twelve signature characteristics, each a portion of the packaging.

I took the assignment, walked out of his office, went to the cafeteria, and stared off in space, trying to formulate my process, and making notes. An hour later I had a plan and went back to brief Bob. He was enthusiastic! Anything I needed was mine! I told him I would get back with him tomorrow at first light with a request for support and an ops order.

At eight A.M. the next morning I presented my plan. We would establish an operation that would collect and examine all packages with ANY of the characteristics. These would be from holdouts in all of the initial parcel processing units. All opening units would have a holdout. Suspect packages would be isolated and moved to our location. I proposed a storage area a distance from the main plant, in case of an accident. For staffing I needed twenty-two volunteers from the parcel unit. The operation would commence in three days and run twenty-four hours a day. Any packages with three of the characteristics would be isolated and given to the FBI, and some logistical details. Bob authorized it immediately and advised I was now a member of the FBI Unabomber Task Force. I gave him the completed ops order and set about making it happen. By the end of the day it was almost, except for the manning, ready. Tomorrow at eight A.M. the first of the volunteers would arrive and we would begin. And so it happened.

As a result my Operation, 232 Bomb, was installed in all mail processing facilities nationwide. We had several packages come close but nothing serious. However, the operation in Minneapolis did isolate one and it was live. I received a commendation and a check for $2,500.

And a short eulogy for one of the greatest soldiers I have had the pleasure of knowing. Brien T. Collins, or B.T. Collins as he preferred.

One day, prior to Veterans Day A group of us retired rats decided to have a ceremony in full uniform at the Mail Facility. I had heard of a 5th SF badly wounded ex-Capt. in town and finally tracked him down. B.T. said he would be glad to speak at our service. Afterwards, we set down and had a beer together and a relationship was formed. He was, at the time, a California Assemblyman and devoted to WEAVE, The California CCC and the CA Vietnam War memorial and was known for his irreverent and sometimes fanatic support for the causes. For the next several years, I worked for and with B.T. The loss of his right fore-arm and leg never bothered him, in fact we went skiing together one winter. He sadly passed in 1993. Along with Bob Sinclair, he was one of the two most alive men I ever knew.

Work, time with the family, occasionally dancing with my beautiful wife, socializing at the Supervisors Association get together and doing whatever PI work I could fit in, and there was quite a bit. I was sched-uled to turn sixty-two in January of 1996 and Jan and I discussed endless possibilities. She also was eligible to retire at the same time. Yes, no, but what about, how are we going to, suppose this happens or that. But in November we decided to pull the plug. We both put in for our re-tirement, and decided what we wanted to do.

Rich and Famous

Jan got the bright idea that we should buy a motor home and live out of that for the rest of our life, renting the condo. I came up with the idea of traveling base to base and selling something, as we had seen vendors do for several years, and perhaps making enough so that we would not have to touch our retirement. We both got excited, did some checking and decided we would sell indian jewelry and my doberman heads, of which we had sold several for $150 to $300.

And we bought a 1994 twenty-eight foot Bounder Motor Home, for cash, drove it a bit, had a few exciting weekends and stored it, ready to go .We were going to pull our Chevy Suburban.

The 20ᵗʰ of January, 1996, was our last day respectively, we said our goodbyes' and promised to write, and the next week we, with Jake, started our great adventure.

I checked with the base and got the procedure for reserving spots in various BXs and received the okay to sell our products. Each BX that we were to visit had to have a RV Park and at least 5,000 military in population. I got a military map with all the information and wrote each Vendor Manager specifying our arrival and departure days.

After a couple weeks I began to get responses. Occasional we would not be scheduled a week, and we would have that week for ourselves. Eventually we got it down where we would work four weeks and be off one. We were booked for a year and our first stop was a favorite, Albuquerque, New Mexico, to buy product. We found several wholesalers and purchased about $3,000 in jewelry, making arrangements to have the wholesalers ship our future needs. Another $300 for display cases and we were ready, in fact the first stop was right there at Kirtland AFB, where we stayed the first two weeks.

We checked in Saturday with the RV managers, who eventually became good friends, as did a lot of the RV and vendor managers. We went in early Monday, met the manager who showed us which kiosk we could have, and gave us the contract. At the end of our contract, we would take it to the cashier's cage with a check for twenty percent, which they charged for their commission.

We spent an average of $200 for gas and taxes, $15 a night for a RV spot and our food bill including Jake, would run about $60 a week. We averaged about $1,600 in sales, our markup normally being one hundred percent, so our net, profit after expense and tax, was about $250. And we were having fun. After we were set up, only one of us had to man the kiosk. The other, with Jake, could loaf, do the laundry, wash the car, go to the commissary, etc. etc. it worked out to be pretty much what we thought it would be.

We traveled and loafed, for almost four years, Grand Canyon, Yosemite, Meteor Crater and many, many more. If it was within fifty miles of a BX we were working, we saw it. And the people were met who were also vendors were, to the most degree, outstanding. And the current definition of 'gypsy's.' And we continued to average a net of $500 a month, or close to it and were happy with that. Jan, Jake, and I were in our environment and having a hell of a good time.

Lara and her husband Matt, with her two boys, Chris and Nick, were staying in the condo while we wandered around, and we would show up perhaps twice a year and spend a few days. During the summer we would take one of the grandsons with us as we worked Washington State., specifically the Ft. Lewis/McChord complex. In fact we taught Chris how to fish one beautiful day on the Ft. Lewis reservation. Returning to Sacramento, we would take the other with us for an equal amount of time.

Several years earlier, we had made a trip down the Baja peninsula to a little town on the east side named Loretto. There we found small lots, one hundred fifty feet by eighty feet, right on the water, being sold by an American corporation in Los Angeles. And we bought one. Our intent was that someday we would build a 'casita' on the sea and retire. We would journey down there several times over the years, once bringing my daughter in law, her daughter and my mother.

One of the events offered was by a German immigrant who operated a two seat powered hang glider I talked Jan and my Mom in taking a ride and so they did.

Jan was first off. She was strapped in the front seat, preflighted, turned around and took off on the sand. Once airborne, they turned around and flew over us waving, with us waving and hollering in return. They made a bank and went out to sea, climbing to about 3,000 feet and we lost sight of them.in the glare of the sun.

About twenty minutes later, back they came, and swopped low over us, Jan waving like mad, turned, landed and taxied up to us. Jan was almost uncontrollable in her excitement. She quickly told of spotting sharks from fifty feet, and a bevy of whales going south, two of them spouting as they passed by. About fifty feet above them.

And so we convinced Mom, who by this time was eighty-six, and she boarded, was strapped in, briefed and off they went. Again, over the whales and sharks, several fishing boats and returned, waving joyfully. I could not convince my in-laws to ride.

And that night we built a bonfire and told stories into the night. The next day, renting a cab, we journeyed into Loreto to check it out.

It was a town of about 4,000, with the appropriate shops, stores and malls. There were, as there is in most Mexican towns and cities numerous vendors. All of us bought something as the day went by. At lunch I met two American ex-GIs that had settled in Loreto, both having an apartment. They said they loved it and they would never go back 'north.'

That night we had supper in our club on the beach and the next day started back.

And back we went, hot on the trail, one BX after another, sightseeing as we went, for about a year more. But tragedy struck. We had noticed that Jake had been moving slowly and very deliberately for a week or so.

As we were loading and getting ready to leave McChord, Jake, who was outside on a leash refused to come in the Bounder. I finally went out and got him to the step but he would not use it. In exasperation, I attempted to shove him in and he snapped and snarled at me. I finally, using a towel, was able to lift him in, and he hobbled to the rear and laid down in his favorite place, at the end of the bed.

It was obvious there was something seriously wrong. He was in great pain and whimpered occasionally when he moved. We drove all night and finally got back to Sacramento in the early hours, and took him to our vet who we had alerted several hour before. Poor Jake hobbled in and we went to the back of the clinic where the vet asked us to wait. We were really worried.

And in a short time, the vet came up front. He said that he regretted telling us this, but Jake had a broken back which was untreatable and incurable. Jan broke down in tears and I stuttered and stammered.

We asked if we could see him one more time and were allowed into the operating room where Jake lay on the floor. We kissed and hugged him and said a sad goodbye. We told the vet to cremate him, I helped Jan back into the motor home and we started home, in dejection and sadness. She was still sobbing as we came through the front door, Lara had met us, and helped get Jan into bed.

A couple days passed and we started out again and had been on the road for about six months. And then one day it came to a halt.

We were asked to raise both Chris and Nick, and of course to do so, meant we had to change our plans. So home we came, put the RV in storage, and settled back into the condo. Jan and I discussed the various school possibilities and she decided she wanted to home school Chris and send Nick off to a more formal environment. And so it was done.

With two extra mouths to feed, it was apparent that we needed a little extra so I tried to resurrect my PI business, and had some luck.

With the advent of the Internet, and the mass availability of information access, the need for PIs had shrunk and many of my friends had moved on to other vocations. And a word of warning to the reader if they are interested in using an online service.

I have, over the years used them all and they all contain information that is incorrect. Be careful about the conclusion you draw from the information, for a fee, that they provided you. Rather than using them as an authority, I use them to generate a lead. Any good investigator will tell you that unless information is confirmed from a second unrelated source, it should be viewed as suspect. And on rare occasion even if confirmed, still wrong.

But right off the bat I contracted with an agency that had a contract with the IRS. They were interested in locating students, and others, who had overstayed their visa. I received at least one assignment a week and that helped a little, but I still needed more to comfortably raise the kids and do right by Jan. I absolutely refused to touch our savings.

One day I received a phone call from a female who said that I had been highly recommended and she had a job for me. We arraigned to meet in a downtown restaurant, not far from the Capitol. We shook hands. She was in her mid 40s, rather attractive, poised, earnest, and a little condescending. I pegged her as someone's secretary, either a major business-man or a politician. The first thing she said was that this job would be sensitive and confidential. She firmly elicited a promise that I would not ever speak a word of this to anyone. Becoming more interested, I agreed.

There was a concern, by some people, that Governor Jerry Brown had been paying the communist Huk organi-zation to leave his tea plantation, in the Philippine's, alone. She would like me to confirm this fact. I responded that I would be glad to investigate the allegation, but the confir-mation, if there was one, would be determined after the in-vestigation was complete. She was a little put back but quickly regained her composure. She said she understood and asked for my rates. I quoted one hundred dollars a day plus ex-penses, and I would like to take another investigator with me. And I told her that the fees were for effort, not deter-mining that the allegation did occur and she nodded. She asked how long it would take, and I replied I had no idea. She stood and said that she would check with me in a couple days, we left the restaurant and I called Pat Jenkins, the other PI. When I told him what I had quoted for our rate, he said, "Hell yeas' let's do the bitch!" I told him to hang tight and I'd be back with him.

When I briefed Jan, she was concerned with the presupposed danger involved. She asked if I were going to 'carry' and I told her I couldn't. I had unofficially, and illegally, been carrying my 1911 when involved in PI work, for several years. But not on an aircraft and certainly not oversees.

The next week, the lady, still unnamed, called me and cancelled the operation. I asked her why and she said she could not comment, but thank you. I called Pat and gave him the bad news and he said, "Oh well."

About this time I saw an ad where the Transportation Security Agency was advertising for a new position at the airport, and I applied and was accepted. I had absolutely no idea what the job was going to be but it was steady and the pay not too bad.

The job was as a screener, in uniform, at the airport. Our job was to check people and carry-on baggage as they came through our checkpoint, a baggage scanning belt and a walk through metal detector. We were on alert for weapons or explosives.

After two weeks of training, we started operations at the Airport, working steady shifts that were eight hours in length. The crew was competent and motivated, 9/11 was fresh in everyone's mind, but our leadership was almost non-existent. And I began to experience some unease.

Because of my background, I started to look around to see if we were truly stopping any terrorist and I came to the conclusion that we were not. No special attention was given to people who were noticeably nervous. Our procedures did not prevent the carrying on of explosives. I estimated that a quarter pound of PETN or C-4 would be enough to rupture at high altitudes, and either could be bodily molded.. And a timer or initiator was a simple matter of a watch or a fountain pen modified internally. So I mentioned these concerns and was told to just "do your job."

After we had been there about two months, and many had asked me about federal benefits and employment because they could not get answers from their TSA bosses. A retired Navy chief and I approached the manager, who happened to be a reserve Brigadier General and in our best military manner, explain the employees concerns. His response, which I have never forgotten was, "Just do as your told, that's all that I want!"

So I formed the 'Wolfpack,' an internet blog established for the purpose of providing information on federal employment and several other areas. Our membership grew and so did the hostility of management for me and the site, with one exception.

His name was Jeff Holmgren, in his mid-forties thin and balding. He was an extremely intelligent man, and happened to be a retired Coast Guard Officer. After a while I could sense he also did not care for the leadership posture of the rest of the staff, but was powerless. Jeff and I hit it off immediately. His family, with a girl and a boy, were on a farm in Washington State and he planned on bringing them down shortly. We would often have long conversations over a number of managerial subjects and understood each other completely.

The Transition

Jeff would occasionally came to the house for supper and we became close friends and this relationship continues to the present day. He has subsequently climbed the ladder of success and is now TSA Director for Washington State, Alaska and Oregon with thirty-five airports under his guidance. Unfortunately his marriage failed and he subsequently remarried Becky, a prominent financial advisor, who lives in Sacramento.

And as I occasionally did, I added to my life. Jan was always interested in the church, and in fact we had been going to our 7th Day Adventist church for several years. And one Saturday, Jan was baptized in the church. It caused me to reexamine my life and its concepts and how much I had changed since marrying her.

In 2004, all of the screeners were given an X-ray interpretation test and I was the only one who failed. I had been having vision problems for a couple years. Jan and I had been getting a Laser treatment which did not last. So, other than the PI work, which even with Mantech, was spasmodic, I was off in search of another job. And additionally, a rude shock.

We received a letter from the LA District Attorney's Office. It explained that Southern California Holding, the broker that was selling lots in Mexico on the Baja, was found, by the Mexican government, to have been engaged in fraudulent and deceitful conduct by underreporting sales and the cost thereof over an extended time, and in essence cheated the Mexican government out of several millions.

Therefore, the Mexican government had rescinded all obligations and rights it had to the holding company and a few other things. In essence the Mexicans had taken back several 'resorts' that people had bought into, quoting the Mexican law that denied foreign ownership of property located on Mexican waters.

The letter concluded stating that a suit had been filed against the holding company and would I care to enter into it? I said yes and signed it, and of course we never heard another peep out of Los Angeles.

We had lost several thousand along with our eventual retirement property. But to counter balance our financial picture, we had paid off the car, had no house payment and in August of 2004, paid off the last of my credit cards and threw them joyfully in the garbage, never using them again. And we had about $20,000 in savings. Our broker of forty years had died in 2002 and we had converted all of our holdings to interest bearing, safe, vehicles.

I thought it would be interesting to drive truck, so I went to school for five weeks, learned the trade and did that for a couple years, one day getting out of the cab, slipping on ice and breaking my shoulder in the fall. After it 'healed' I found that it was very difficult to turn the steering wheel, so I quit and went back to my school, where they hired me on as Chief Instructor.

The first thing that went wrong was the pay. I was promised a pay computed in one manner, my actual pay was computed differently, causing a forty dollar a week difference. I had been hired by the operations chief and had never met the owner. I felt that a projector was necessary for the students to understand more clearly, he did not. I ask him for writing board erasers, and his reply was 'use paper towels.' On Saturdays, I would take the class to the yard, where trucks were staged and we taught the practical stuff. This Saturday the roads leading there were closed and we could not gain access, so I turned the students around and gave them the day off. When he heard, he snarled that I "should have been smart enough to discover that in advance."

I said, "—— you," and quit on the spot.

My last little formal employment, in 2012, was as a substitute teacher. They made good money and I loved to teach, and always had. Besides, they said that based on my performance after six months, I could apply as a full time teacher. Which I thought was great, because they really made a good living and I would love my work. I went to the college and got my certification, came back and reported ready for work.

In the meantime, Mantech advised me that they had lost their contract and they were "moving on without my services."

The first week I received only two calls to sub, both more of a security monitor than a teacher. The second week, two actual teaching gigs in a middle school class, the next week four. And by the third month I was busy. The teacher you were subbing for was supposed to leave you an outline, but occasionally that did not happen, and then I was on my own. And on occasion I ignored the outline and after talking to the kids, taught what I thought they needed. I was criticized for that. On occasion, after teaching a class, the kids would stand and clap, almost never heard of. I loved what I was doing and I was apparently damn good at it. It had got to the point that teachers would call me at home asking me specifically, to sub for them.

It came time for me to apply and I did, receiving the recommendations of three principals. Time went by and I finally went to personnel to find out what the delay was. I was told I was not hirable because I had a service connected disability and the district did not want to take responsibility if it worsened. I quit in disgust.

I went home and checked the books. I was making fifty-five thousand in retirement and Jan was bringing in another seven thousand, and we had no bills.

I retired, for the fourth time, on the spot, and in fact lost interest in the PI business, letting my license, which I had since 1976, lapse. In 2012.

And here I want to enter some information in a nonstandard manner.

In 2004, I was listening to the radio in my car when a group came on and sang a song. I was so moved I had to move over on the shoulder to listen to it.

I was listening to a new group called El Divo, Italian for divine partner. I researched and found they were four multi-national young men that sang a classical crossover style which became known as 'classpop' or classical music done in a pop style. They are absolutely outstanding! In 2002 Simon Cromwell heard them sing individually and joined them together. They sing in the style of Pavarotti, Domingo and the other classical tenors. I have their CD in my car and in my stereo at home and I play them consistently I told Jan that if they ever appeared within 500 miles, we would attend their concert and this has occurred three times.

In 2009, one morning in November on a Saturday morning I was lying in bed, having my third cup of coffee and watching the CBS News, when I heard "Travis Air Force Base" and looked up.

On the report was an announcement that at ten a.m, Code Pink, founded and possessed by Cindy Sheehan, would protest the use of guided weapons to kill civilians in Iraq. I had heard of Mrs. Sheehan, who tragically had lost a son in Iraq a couple years prior. They then showed one of the clips where she said that the missiles fired by the military were intentional targeted against the civilian population. In her tirade she neglected to mention that the civilians in fact, were the same international terrorists that had killed her son.

And I said to myself, "This is bullshit, not on my beloved Travis."

So I dug out the uniform, a little snug, laced up the jump boots, grabbed my beret and off to Travis I went. And on the way down the thought hovered in my mind that the Air Force takes a dim view of people in uniform attending political events. "Screw it, I gotta do this."

As I pulled in, I could see the demonstration had been moved a short distance from the main gate, to the visitor registrations complex. There were a crowd of perhaps 200, a couple buses, several police cars and Air Police vehicles parked in the parking areas.

As I got out of my car, one of the CHP Officers asked me if others were coming and I responded, "Hell no, there's only one demonstration to deal with, one combat controller is all that's needed."

The crowd was in high spirits, banners waving and Cindy, with a bull horn, was egging them on. I approached the crowd and could see that they had arranged their ranks so that the ladies were up front and the men in the rear.

I hollered that, "You are all full of shit and that these demonstrations were, in fact, not supportive of the troops, but in fact ridiculed the servicemen. The missiles were targeted at either terrorists or terrorist support facilities." I further shouted that, "You assholes need to be waving flags and supporting the military which defends your own right of protest!"

By this time Mrs. Sheehan had put her bullhorn in my face and I knocked it aside. She did not try it again, but our conversation got to be nose to nose. Turning to the group, I referred to the men in the rear as "chickenshits" and dared any or all to "come on up." None of them ventured forth.

An Air Police T.Sgt. moved into the crowd and asked me respectively if I would accompany him and I replied, "Sure." We moved up and away from the demonstrators, who were now finishing up. One of the police offices came over and said. "Well done Sergeant, I'm an ex-Marine," and with a grin, said, "watch what happens next."

The local police and the CHP began issuing citations to every vehicle and the demonstrator's buses, citing them all for illegal parking! Cindy Sheehan was furious and threatened to sue us all. I was laughing and the police officers were struggling to conceal their smiles. The last I heard of Cindy she was camped out on President George Bush's access road in Texas.

That night I was stunned when the six o'clock news came on and there I was on CBS, face to face with the bullhorn. If you Google "Travis AFB" it is still being carried. And I, for the next several days, received many positive phone calls, one after another, from old friends all over the US.

The Air Force never did frown in my direction.

After the fifteen minutes of fame from Travis, my life seemed to slow and take on substance. Jan and I settled into the business off being grandparents and continuing to raise Chris and Nick.

And by this time, the difference in the boy's personality was evident. Chris was intelligent, outspoken, aggressive and vocal. Nick on the other hand was also intelligent, and in addition, introspective, quiet and thoughtful. Both had been studying Karate for a couple years and both earned their black belts, so we had three black belt holders in the household.

And when Nick was ten, he wrote two articles, one a children's magazine and another for a scholarship committee, and had both articles published in nationwide magazines. And two years later, he joined a soccer team at his school and was first string and a hell of a soccer player. Nick was a distinguished high school graduate and enrolled in college to become a veterinarian, and still lives with us.

We did not have a dobie at this point as both Chris and Nick filled that void. Chris brought home a brindle pup and asked if he could stay awhile. This of course turned into several years until Roxie died in 2017. And she was and is sorely missed in my house. A couple years after Roxie arrived, Nick went to the pound and found a little white Pomeranian pup and brought her home, naming him Archie. He has, in reality, became Jan's dog and they go everywhere together.

Chris and his mother had moved to Tennessee and stayed there through his high school graduation and then returned to us in Sacramento. After a period of wandering and unsureness common to teenagers, he decided he wanted to join the Navy and he became a submariner. And a couple years later married and operates out of Groton Ct.

As things do, relationships between us and the kids sometimes were a little strained, caused in part by their lifestyle selection. But out of respect, they never brought this home to roost. Like all parents, we eventually understood and accepted their choices. Once and awhile the kids would need financial help and like all parents we acceded. All in all the time was uneventful, full and loving for Jan and I. Our financial position was excellent and we loved each other deeply…and we were even taking dancing lessons! And regarding these, my favorite, the tango, is first on the list.

Life was good.

David and his partner, Mike, came down for a visit and spent some time with us. If was all fun and enjoyable. In fact, as I have mentioned, I am going to enclose a genealogy chart with this book so that the grandkids have some idea where they came from.

And lo and behold, Steve's angel appeared. He received a back pay social security check which allowed him to buy, for cash, a house and property in Kansas, and in addition he has decided to go into the custom jewelry business from his home.

Through a series of mishaps and reversals, in mid-2017 Lara and Mike moved in with us and they have two large dogs. We now have to shut Archie off if the dogs have to go to the bathroom but that's okay, Mike and Lara help out a great deal and are continually searching for a place of their own.

And in April of 2016, the transition became complete when I was baptized in our 7th Day Adventists church.

I look back on this manuscript, still unsure of whether or not I want to publish and see a life which began as evil and counterintuitive, and eventually, with a great deal of help from others, reached a plateau of understanding, both of others and myself...I did it my way.

Combat Control Teams

Combat Control Teams (CCT) (AFSC 1C2X1) are ground combat forces assigned to Special Tactics Squadrons (STS) within the Air Force Special Operations Command (AFSOC). The mission of a Combat Controller is to deploy by the most feasible means available into combat and non-permissive environments. Combat Controllers are Special Tactics Operators who establish assault zones, while simultaneously providing: Air Traffic Control, Fire support, and Command and Control Communications in the joint arena. Additionally, Combat Controllers expertly employ all-terrain vehicles, amphibious vehicles, weapons and demolitions. Functions include assault zone assessment and establishment; air traffic control; command and control communications; special operations terminal attack control; and removal of obstacles with demolitions. The CCTs provide a unique capability and deploy with joint air and ground forces in the execution of Direct Action, Counter-Terrorism, Foreign Internal Defense, Humanitarian assistance, Special Reconnaissance, Austere Airfield, and Combat Search and Rescue operations.

Combat Control Teams (CCTs) originated during the airborne campaign of World War II. Major parachute assaults fell well short of expectations, resulting in some cases with personnel being air dropped as much as 30 miles from their intended target areas. The shortcomings of these operations identified the need for effective guidance and control of air transported combat forces. Thus, a small parachute scout company of Army pathfinders was organized and trained. Their mission was to precede the main assault force to an objective area and, through the use of high powered lights, flares and smoke pots, provide visual guidance and critical weather information to inbound aircraft.

In 1943, pathfinders were first employed during the airborne reinforcement of allied troops in Italy. Later, pathfinders from the 101st and 82nd Airborne Divisions played an integral role in the Normandy invasion.

After the establishment of the U.S. Air Force as a separate service on 18 September 1947, organizational changes resulted in tactical airlift and aerial port squadrons assuming responsibility for support of the U.S. Army ground forces. Air Force pathfinder teams, later called combat control teams, were activated in January of 1953 to provide navigational aids and air traffic control for the growing airlift forces. They were incorporated into aerial port squadrons and remained there until 1977, when they were assigned to the Director of Operations. In 1984 combat control was restructured into a system of squadrons and detachments reporting directly to numbered Air Forces and in 1991 they were placed under the control of host wing commanders.

Combat Controllers and Pararescuemen must be capable of deploying by the most advantageous means into their mission areas. For this reason, a variety of deployment techniques are used by both specialties. The level of training you receive in certain deployment methods will be dependent upon the unit you are assigned. However, most of these deployment capabilities will be taught during initial training

- parachute operations (Jumpmaster directed spotting for accuracy)
- Static line (low altitude)
- With combat equipment
- With SCUBA equipment
- Into forested areas
- Into vast bodies of water

High Altitude Low Opening (military free fall)

- With combat equipment
- With oxygen

High Altitude High Opening (cross country canopy flight)

- With combat equipment
- With oxygen

Waterborne Infiltration's

- SCUBA/Draegger
- Submarine lock-outs
- Aircraft boat drops
- Rubber Raiding Craft operations
- Scout (surface) swimming

Mountain Operations

- Rock/ice climbing
- Rappelling
- High angle evacuations

Helicopter Operations

- Rappelling
- Fast rope

- Rope Ladder
- Hoist operations (PJs)
- Gunner/scanner (PJs)

Overland Movement

- Motorcycles
- All Terrain Vehicles (ATVs)
- Motor vehicle
- Team navigation

Arctic Operations

- Cross country skiing
- Downhill skiing
- Skijoring
- Snowmobiles
- Snowshoes
- Akhio

Combat Control Prerequisites

- Be a volunteer
- Be a US Citizen
- Be a male (based on current Department of Defense policies)
- Have a general score of at least 43 on the Armed Services Vocational Aptitude Battery test
- Have vision of best eye 20/70, worst eye 20/100; correctable to 20/20. (No Radial Keratotomy.)
- Have normal color vision
- Meet specific physical fitness standards
- Be a proficient swimmer
- Be a High School graduate or have a GED

- Able to obtain a SECRET security clearance
- Successful completion of the PAST test
- Minimum physical profile (PULHES) of 111111 (no problems)
- Pass an Initial flying class III physical qualification of aircrew, parachute, and maritime diving duty
- Strength aptitude standard of "K" for retention of AFSC

Combat Control Orientation Course introduces airmen to Combat Control history, missions, and career field specific skills. Students are required to participate in a rigorous physical fitness program that introduces them to physical exercises that are conducted during the pipeline. The course includes the following events: running, swimming, calisthenics, weight training, sports nutrition, sports medicine, M-16/M-9 weapons qualification, CPR qualification, and Combat Control related skills. Upon graduation, students attend the following pipeline courses: ATC – Air Traffic Control School 15.5 weeks, US Army Airborne Parachutist 3 weeks, US Air Force Combat Survival 2.5 weeks, US Air Force Underwater Egress Training 1 day, and Combat Control School 13 weeks (AFSC awarding course).

Combat controllers are among the most highly trained personnel in the U.S. military. They maintain air traffic control qualification skills throughout their careers; many qualify and maintain currency in joint terminal attack control procedures, in addition to other special operations skills. Their 35-week training and unique mission skills earn them the right to wear the scarlet beret.

Combat Control Orientation Course, Lackland Air Force Base, TX: This two-week orientation course focuses on sports physiology, nutrition, basic exercises, CCT history and fundamentals.

Combat Control Operator Course, Keesler AFB, MS: This 15 ½ - week course teaches aircraft recognition and performance, air navigation aids, weather, airport traffic control, flight assistance service, communication procedures, conventional approach control, radar procedures and air traffic rules. This is the same course that all Air Force air traffic controllers attend and is the heart of a combat controller's job.

U.S. Army Airborne School, Fort Benning, GA: This three-week course teaches basic parachuting skills required to infiltrate an objective area by static line airdrop.

U.S. Air Force Basic Survival School, Fairchild AFB, WA: This two-and-a-half-week course teaches basic survival techniques for remote areas. Instruction includes principles, procedures, equipment and techniques, which enables individuals to survive, regardless of climatic conditions or unfriendly environments and return home.

Combat Control School, Pope AFB, NC: This 13-week course provides final CCT qualifications. Training includes physical training, small unit tactics, land navigation, communications, assault zones, demolitions, fire support and field operations including parachuting. At the completion of this course, each graduate is awarded the 3-skill level (journeymen), scarlet beret and CCT flash.

Special Tactics Advanced Skills Training, Hurlburt Field, FL: Advanced Skills Training (AST) is a 12-to-15-month program for newly assigned combat controller operators. AST produces mission-ready operators for the Air Force and United States Special Operations Command. The AST schedule is broken down into four phases: water, ground, employment, and full mission profile. The course tests the trainee's personal limits through demanding mental and physical training. Combat controllers also attend the following schools during AST:

U.S. Army Military Free Fall Parachutist School, Fort Bragg, N.C., and Yuma Proving Grounds, AZ: This course instructs trainees in free fall parachuting procedures. The five-week course provides wind tunnel training, in-air instruction focusing on student stability, aerial maneuvers, air sense, parachute opening procedures and parachute canopy control.

U.S. Air Force Combat Divers School, Panama City, FL: Trainees become combat divers, learning to use scuba and closed circuit diving equipment to covertly infiltrate denied areas. The four-week course provides training to depths of 130 feet, stressing development of maximum underwater mobility under various operating conditions.

U.S. Navy Underwater Egress Training, Pensacola Naval Air Station, FL: This course teaches how to safely escape from an aircraft that has ditched in the water. The one-day instruction includes principles, procedures and techniques necessary to get out of a sinking aircraft.

Note: This article was copied from SHADOWSPEAR, the SPE-COPS website for Jan 30 2009.

Epilogue

As always in my life, there is constant change and challenge. Since I finished the book, Jan and I have renewed acquaintances With Joyce' Jones, my lovely and loved adopted sister's family, Ron Jones, etc. and I have ventured forward a little advice that I hope helps their family.. Nick, after being laid off, has decided to, like his brother, join the Navy with hopes of becoming a Computer Technician. We are not patiently waiting for the Navy to get off it's ass and complete his processing.

We will see what transpires. Read the next chapter and see what force molded me…. …that's all she wrote, folks….